Real School Issues

Real School Issues

Case Studies for Educators

Edited by Laura Trujillo-Jenks and
Rebecca Ratliff Fredrickson

ROWMAN & LITTLEFIELD
Lanham • Boulder • New York • London

Published by Rowman & Littlefield
A wholly owned subsidiary of The Rowman & Littlefield Publishing Group, Inc.
4501 Forbes Boulevard, Suite 200, Lanham, Maryland 20706
www.rowman.com

Unit A, Whitacre Mews, 26-34 Stannary Street, London SE11 4AB

Copyright © 2017 by Laura Trujillo-Jenks and Rebecca Ratliff Fredrickson

All rights reserved. No part of this book may be reproduced in any form or by any electronic or mechanical means, including information storage and retrieval systems, without written permission from the publisher, except by a reviewer who may quote passages in a review.

British Library Cataloguing in Publication Information Available

Library of Congress Cataloging-in-Publication Data

Names: Trujillo-Jenks, Laura, editor. | Fredrickson, Rebecca Ratliff, editor.
Title: Real school issues : case studies for educators / edited by Laura Trujillo-Jenks and Rebecca Ratliff Fredrickson.
Description: Lanham, Maryland : Rowman and Littlefield, 2017. | Includes bibliographical references and index.
Identifiers: LCCN 2017007779 (print) | LCCN 2017016423 (ebook) | ISBN 9781475831399 (electronic) | ISBN 9781475831375 (cloth : alk. paper) | ISBN 9781475831382 (pbk. : alk. paper)
Subjects: LCSH: School management and organization—United States—Case studies. | Educational change—United States—Case studies.
Classification: LCC LB2805 (ebook) | LCC LB2805 .R365 2017 (print) | DDC 371.2—dc23
LC record available at https://lccn.loc.gov/2017007779

∞ ™ The paper used in this publication meets the minimum requirements of American National Standard for Information Sciences Permanence of Paper for Printed Library Materials, ANSI/NISO Z39.48-1992.

Printed in the United States of America

Contents

Introduction	vii
I: Issues That Affect the Classroom	**1**
1 Poor Classroom Management and the First Year Teacher *Sarah K. McMahan*	3
2 Investigating the Demands and Challenges of Critical Thinking Instruction *Gina Anderson and Jody Piro*	17
3 Academic Support and Motivation during Second Language Acquisition: Serious Considerations for Educators *Melinda T. Cowart and Savanna Doroodchi*	31
II: Issues That Affect the School Campus	**47**
4 The American-Type International School: A Question of Ethics *Warren G. Ortloff, Luz Marina Escobar, and Ava Muñoz*	49
5 The Teacher and the Second Job *Laura Trujillo-Jenks and Rebecca Ratliff Fredrickson*	67
6 Innovation and State Testing: The Challenges of a University Charter School *Wesley D. Hickey and Joanna Neel*	81
7 Psychosocial Factors Impacting Bullying in a School Context: Responses for Campus Safety *Shannon R. Scott, Kathy DeOrnellas, and Lisa H. Rosen*	91

III: Issues That Affect the School's Relationship with Stakeholders   **101**

  8 Autism Spectrum Disorder: Sophie's Journey   103
     Karen L. Dunlap

  9 Every Student Counts: Did She Really Say That?   117
     Teresa Starrett

 10 Teaching Students to Learn or Teaching to the Test?   125
     Patrick M. Jenlink

 11 Purpose, Processes, and Change: Issues Parents and Stakeholders Bring to Schools   145
     Peggy Malone

Appendix A: Discussion Protocol   157

Appendix B: Universal Intellectual Standards Quick Reference Guide   159

Appendix C: Seven Steps for Jigsaw Socrates Café and Graphic Organizer   161

Index   169

About the Editors   177

About the Contributors   179

Introduction

Case studies are fun to use! Through case studies, critical thinking, deeper thinking, higher order thinking, and reflective thinking can occur. Hence, this book is full of fun learning that also allows for thought-provoking discussions because it contains case studies that will help all who read them critically think about the different issues that can be found on school campuses across the nation.

We created this book with both the practicing and preservice educator in mind. For the practitioner, this book is a good choice for a book study because the issues found in each case study may be easily attributed to a campus. The issues presented could be discussed and worked through, which then could become a platform or plan of action for a real-life issue at a school. Working through the case studies create a safe way to discuss ways to work through difficult situations.

For preservice teachers and administrators, this book is an excellent resource for any undergraduate or graduate course. When reading each case study and understanding each issue, a preservice educator is one step closer to understanding the real-world issues that can be found in schools. Having case studies to work through will help preservice educators talk through difficult issues without feeling nervous about retaliation or making a wrong decision.

A group of professors, who have all spent time in public education, have written a chapter/case study that focuses on a certain aspect of school. Some case studies include ethical issues, while others focus on curriculum issues. Still others deal with a multitude of issues that encompass more than one theme. When you read through each case study, you will see the expertise of these professors as their knowledge is illuminated throughout the different sections of each chapter.

As you work through each chapter, you will find different sections. The first section is the *Case Study*, which is preceded by a brief introduction to the chapter. In the case study, you will meet the key characters and you will read through the different issues that are presented. Important information will be presented that will give reason to the characters, along with a problem or an issue that will need to be solved.

The next section will be *The Literature Review*. Some literature reviews will be presented along with insights from the authors. Each chapter/case study has either happened to the author or has been a part of a research project for the author. Because of this, the authors of each chapter will present personal insight concerning the topics and issues presented throughout the case study. A reference section at the end of the chapter is provided.

The third section is the *Guiding Questions*; a set of questions that relates to the case study and literature review is offered. These questions are to help you critically think, think deeper, think at a higher order, and reflectively think. Along with the last section, *Final Considerations*, which are final thoughts given about the case study, literature review, and guiding questions, allow for application of knowledge.

This book will allow undergraduate/graduate students and practicing educators the opportunity to explore, discuss, and examine multiple scenarios in education. Also, this book will allow for both contemplation of how to understand and consider different solutions for a particular issue, as well as consideration regarding how to choose deliberate professional growth opportunities that focus on specific growth needs. As preservice and practicing educators use this book, they will be more prepared to work with all persons present on a campus in meaningful ways.

I

Issues That Affect the Classroom

Chapter One

Poor Classroom Management and the First Year Teacher

Sarah K. McMahan

In the case study that follows, a new teacher is faced with a nightmare when her contract is nonrenewed. The lack of mentoring and the need to navigate through her first year of teaching without guidance leads to chaos in the classroom. Being a first year teacher is tough, but being a first year teacher without support is nearly impossible.

THE CASE STUDY

The First Year Teacher

Ms. Moore recently graduated from college and two weeks after graduation she was offered a 7th grade math position at Bonham Middle School. She was familiar with Bonham faculty and students since she completed her student teaching assignment in 6th grade at the school. During the summer months, Ms. Moore attended all the Math Professional Development workshops the district offered. Moreover, she attended with her 7th grade team the Professional Learning Community (PLCs) conference.

As the beginning of school approached, Ms. Moore feverishly worked on her classroom and prepping for the school year. Her team was thrilled to have her since she was a top-notch university student who had great rapport with the students, had a solid understanding of the content, and had exhibited positive classroom management strategies during her student teaching experience.

The school year started and Ms. Moore implemented effective procedures and routines. She learned that good classroom management entailed being consistent in routines and rules. During the first few weeks of school, she had minimal discipline problems. Most of the discipline issues were related to students using their phones when they were not supposed to, tardiness, and constant talking episodes with a few students. All but a handful of these problem students were in extracurricular activities (i.e., sports, ROTC, student council), so their behaviors were easy to curtail once she visited with their sponsor/coach about the students' behavior. She quickly learned with the other few behavioral issue type students that she could not send them to the office because they did not listen or follow instructions. For example, students texted continually even when asked repeatedly to put up their phone. The office would send them back with the response "you need to find ways to deal with this issue in your class."

After a few times of the students getting sent back to class after the assistant principal (Mr. Selman) did "nothing," she figured out she better find some ways to handle these students' minor issues. She had a great relationship with her team and they were able to give her ideas/tips to curtail these problem students' behaviors. It worked mostly, and throughout the first semester it was a trial-and-error approach to redirecting problematic student behaviors. Overall, Ms. Moore navigated the demands of a first year teacher quite well at the end of the first semester. However, things began to spiral downhill after coming back from the holiday break and starting the second semester.

The Issue(s)

Ms. Moore was excited to be back at school and in the routine after a relaxing holiday break. The first week back went smoothly—no major management issues, just the typical redirecting behaviors and re-engaging the students' focus after a few weeks of not being in school. Then, on the second week of the second semester, a new student, Greg, transferred into the school district from a neighboring state.

During team planning time that week where she was able to spend time with her grade-level team, the team reviewed the student's permanent file to gain insight into his academic performance and behavior issues. There were no documented circumstances of expulsion from school; only two times during his 6th grade year was he in in-school suspension for defiant behavior and verbal assault (cursing at his teacher). His file indicated that he was a B student who usually made As in elective classes, Bs in core classes except math, where he usually was a C student. The past state assessment (two years ago) showed that he met the required academic standard, but just barely in math and reading.

Armed with this knowledge, the team decided that they would administer benchmark assessment tests during the next week to gain more information on his academic performance in each subject. This information would assist the team and individual teachers in meeting his academic needs.

In an attempt to build a positive relationship with the student and parents, Ms. Moore emailed both parents to establish positive lines of communication.

> Dear Parents/Guardians of Greg,
> Welcome to Bonham Middle School. Your son has just enrolled in my 7th grade math course. We are currently studying Quadratic Formulas these nine weeks. I keep my webpage on the school portal updated weekly with events, assignments, project due dates, and curriculum documents. I also send weekly announcements, via listserve, to all students' parents/guardians with reminders and important weekly information. Please take a few minutes to review my site and acclimate yourself with the scope of the course, as well as review other team information. I look forward to working with your son the rest of the year. Please let me know if you have any questions.

Both parents were quick to respond and compliment Ms. Moore for taking time to reach out and connect with them.

> Dear Ms. Moore,
> Thank you for the email. We appreciate you taking time out of your busy day to welcome us and our son to Bonham Middle School. We will visit the team's webpage and your own (math) page often. Now that we can review the webpages, we can stay informed of what is happening at school and help him.
>
> Our son is a good kid who does not always apply himself. His strong area is not math, so he will need lots of practice and help in order to make good grades this year. We tell him often that he could be retained in the grade if he doesn't make the grades, so he needs to apply himself.
>
> Again, we appreciate you reaching out to us. Please continue to keep us posted on his progress.

A week later, after reviewing the benchmark results for Greg in all content areas at the team meeting, the team agreed that Greg needed additional support to get up to grade level in math and reading content knowledge. Ms. Moore and Mrs. Michelson, the English teacher, agreed to send an email to his parents requesting that Greg attend tutorials for English and math each week. Greg's mom responds:

> Teachers,
> I think tutorials will be beneficial for Greg as he needs to catch up on skills in English and math. We will make sure he stays after school for tutorials on Tuesdays and Thursdays so he can get on track in your classes.

The next week, Greg attended tutorials for Ms. Moore and Mrs. Michelson two times a week. Ms. Moore found that Greg was behind, but she was confident that tutorials would help him get up to par before the end of the school year. Ms. Moore continued the next five weeks with tutoring Greg. She noticed that Greg worked hard and applied himself during tutorials, but in class he was disengaged and didn't want to do anything. His daily grades suffered and she communicated this information to his parents.

Throughout the next few weeks, Greg continued to slack off in class, yet he attended tutorials and seemed to be progressing in math and English. This continued until the next school break. After spring break, Ms. Moore noticed that Greg refused to do anything in class and started causing disruptions that got other students off task. He also intentionally defied Ms. Moore in front of other students.

Ms. Moore reverted to her consistent approach to daily procedures and implemented her steps in her behavioral plan to contain Greg's disruptions. She even conducted phone conferences with Greg's mom regarding his behavior. During a parent phone conference, Greg's mom revealed that Greg had become increasingly aggressive and withdrawn from school, his friends, and even her. She mentioned that she and Greg's dad separated over the winter holidays and this had caused a negative change in Greg's disposition and behavior.

After the parent/teacher phone call, Ms. Moore consulted with her team and they each stated that Greg was withdrawn and moody in their class; however, they said he was not causing behavior problems, he was just withdrawn, had stopped doing homework, and rarely participated in class. Her team helped Ms. Moore come up with a game plan to address Greg's defiance in her class and she began to implement it.

The next day while Ms. Moore passed out papers, Greg blurted out in a loud angry voice "Damn Miss. Why you giving us more f***ing work to do? This is crap!" Ms. Moore was taken aback by his outburst and was lost for words as to how to respond to him. She had never had a student curse directly at her or aloud in front of the whole class. Ms. Moore immediately told Greg to "get up and go out to the hallway now." He shook his head in disgust, but got up from his seat and went to the hall. Ms. Moore told the other students in the class to "Take one of these worksheets and work by yourself on it." She then walked out the door, closed it, but peeked through the window to watch her class as she began the following conversation with Greg.

"What was that in there? What happened and why are you so angry?" He responded, "Nothing, Miss. I just hate this school and this class. You are always making me do stuff that I don't understand." Ms. Moore responded, "I am sorry you feel this way, but this is school and you are here to learn and follow directions. You cannot just lose your temper and cuss at me when you don't like something. Now head down to the principal's office and I will email your referral."

Greg headed to the principal's office and Ms. Moore went back into her room to write the referral. Once the referral was emailed, she started back with her class and tried to re-engage them as they moved on from the incident. Even though she was flustered and upset, she tried her best to continue to teach and to work with her students.

All of sudden she noticed Greg peeking through the door window and making faces at his classmates. Ms. Moore walked over to the door, opened the door, and told Greg to "get moving to the office." Greg said "Whatever b**ch!" and walked away. Ms. Moore then closed the door behind her as she stood in the hallway where Greg was so her students would not hear. She then said, "Get back over here now. I am so tired of your s**t. Get your a** to the principal now."

Greg turned and walked toward the office and Ms. Moore noticed Mrs. Klein (the art teacher) was twelve feet behind her. She didn't acknowledge Mrs. Klein—she just walked back into her classroom, shut the door, and told the students to finish up what they were doing and wait for the bell.

That afternoon she got an email from Mr. Selman (the assistant principal) asking her to come visit with him after school. Ms. Moore went down to visit with him and found the principal (Mrs. Gordon) and the art teacher (Mrs. Klein) also sitting and waiting for her in the meeting. As the meeting started, Mr. Selman asked Ms. Moore to recount the event with Greg. She told him the details of the incident with Greg, but failed to mention that she cursed at him. Then Mr. Selman asked if Ms. Moore used volatile language at Greg. Ms. Moore, anxious and emotional over the event said,

> Yes. I lost it with him today. I have been trying so hard to help him since he is a struggling student. I have been in contact with his mom regarding his academic performance, I have tutored him, I have asked my team for assistance in dealing with his change in behavior and I don't know what happened to this kid. He disengaged himself and this turned into inappropriate behavior and he cursed at me in front of the class today. I was so shocked. No kid has ever done that to me and it totally caught me off guard. I then went outside and told him to go to the office. He didn't go and I went back out to the hall and went off on him. (Crying) I know it was not professional to handle him with curse language. It is unprofessional and uncalled for. I am sorry.

Mr. Selman and Mrs. Gordon reiterated the importance of showing professionalism even under stressful events with students. Mr. Selman acknowledged that he too has handled issues involving students cursing at him with unprofessionalism in circumstances and that had negative implications. Mrs. Gordon stated she would document this instance (as is standard protocol) and it would be part of her yearly summative evaluation.

Additionally, Mr. Selman and Mrs. Gordon stated that Greg's parents needed to be informed of the incident and an apology to them, as well as

Greg, needed to be completed by the end of the week. Mr. Selman and Mrs. Gordon suggested that a conference be scheduled with administrators and the parents.

The conference was arranged for Friday before school and consisted of Greg's mom and dad, Mr. Selman, Ms. Moore, Mrs. Gordon, Mrs. Brant (the team leader), and the school counselor. Ms. Moore begun the conference by providing documentation of Greg's behavioral changes in her class and was followed by Mrs. Brant's notes regarding Ms. Moore discussing these incidents in team meetings. Mrs. Brant pointed out that Ms. Moore willingly sought mentoring support from colleagues in order to address changes in Greg.

She further stated, "I am not Ms. Moore's official mentor, but I have been coaching her throughout the year on issues. She has made a good faith effort to seek assistance in various instructional and management areas."

The conference conversation then addressed the instance where Greg used aggressive and obscene language in class and toward Ms. Moore. Greg's mom interjected "He told me that he never said any curse words at you, but he did acknowledge he disobeyed you and was defiant." Ms. Moore referred back to the situation detailing exactly the events of the day. Mr. Selman confirmed that Greg did indeed curse at Ms. Moore since it was noted on the office referral. Greg's mom argued that "her son doesn't make up stuff" and he "does not use that language at all." However, Mrs. Gordon interjected that "kids don't always tell the truth to their parents" and that "the issue is not about he said/she said; the purpose of the conference is to inform you of events that transpired with Ms. Moore and Greg."

With that, Mrs. Gordon moved the conversation forward by suggesting that Ms. Moore tell the entire course of events that transpired. As Ms. Moore told the part about her using profanity, she apologized profusely to Greg's mom for using vulgar language at her son and allowing her temper to get the best of her. Greg's mom accepted the apology but stated, "You are unprofessional and need to be written up for exhibiting such behavior." Ms. Moore nodded and Mrs. Gordon interjected, "She has been written up for this occurrence and all supporting documentation will be kept in her personnel file." The meeting concluded with Greg's mom requesting that Greg be placed with another math teacher.

After the conference ended, Ms. Moore went back to her classroom to prepare for the day. Still agitated and upset over the situation, she tried to focus on the project the students in her class were doing. School started as usual and went smoothly up until lunch when she saw the art teacher (Mrs. Klein) at the copy machine.

The art teacher said to Ms. Moore "I hope you learned your lesson. You can't talk to students that way and expect to stay a teacher." Ms. Moore was taken back by the comments and didn't respond. She nodded and left the copy room. Ms. Moore was troubled by the unwarranted comment but didn't say anything to her team or administrator because she didn't want to start more drama.

The Consequences

The weekend finally came and Ms. Moore decided to go to happy hour with her nonteacher friends to blow off some steam after school on Friday night. They met up at the local On the Border for happy hour. After a few drinks, Ms. Moore began to tell her nonteacher friends about all the stuff going on with school and the incident with Greg.

Ms. Moore proceeded to go into detail that "the kid is a sh*t and his mom refuses to accept it." She also said that the art teacher was a nark and "stuff hit the fan because of that stupid old lady who tattled." She proceeded to give more details before the conversation turned to another subject. In the conversation with her friends, Ms. Moore mentioned Greg and Mrs. Klein by name.

Tuesday following the weekend, she received an email from Mrs. Gordon asking her to visit with her after school. Ms. Moore stopped by the principal's office where Mrs. Gordon asked her about her activities on Friday at On the Border. Ms. Moore told her that she went out to dinner with friends and "that's about it." Mrs. Klein then proceeded to tell her that someone reported to her that "you were out drinking with friends on Friday evening and talking about the incident at school last week."

Mrs. Gordon stated that it was reported to her that Ms. Moore called Greg a sh*t and said "other negative things about him and his parents." Ms. Moore was taken back that Mrs. Gordon knew so many of the details but admitted that did occur. Ms. Moore proceeded to ask Mrs. Gordon if she saw her at the restaurant. Mrs. Gordon responded, "No, but Mrs. Klein heard you. She is in my Sunday school class at church and she told about it at church on Sunday." Ms. Moore, biting her lip and in shock, responded with "Oh. Okay." Furthermore, she apologized for talking about a student outside of school in a public place. Mrs. Gordon said, "Well this is another incident I have to document in your file."

Ms. Moore, upset and agitated, said "So that means I have two strikes now on my file. Does that mean I am getting fired"? Mrs. Gordon responded, "No, but I will need to put you on a growth plan. I will call Human Resources and ask to start the process for a growth plan. Once I talk with them and find out the procedures, I will let you know when we'll need to meet about the objectives that we will create for your plan."

After the meeting, she left school and decided to go home and really examine life and if she wanted to continue teaching. Thankfully, Ms. Moore finally caught a break and no other incidents occurred the remaining weeks of school until the summative evaluation conference in mid-May. She never heard back from Mrs. Gordon about her "growth plan" and just thought she forgot about it. Ms. Moore wasn't about to bring that up to her since she knew it had negative implications.

At the summative conference with Mrs. Gordon, specific feedback was given regarding her student performance, her professional performance, and overall evaluation during the first year. Mrs. Gordon praised her for her instructional techniques and commitment to "going above and beyond to help struggling students." (Ms. Moore knew that the two incidents wouldn't earn her high marks, but overall she felt she did a great job her first year.)

Mrs. Gordon noted that her two documented circumstances (cursing at Greg and sharing personal information about Greg in public) earned her an "Unsatisfactory" rating in the Professionalism category. Overall, her total evaluation points equated to "Meets Standards."

She was shocked when Mrs. Gordon said "since you are on a probationary contract being a first year teacher, you are on a one-year contract. We will not be offering you a contract for next year due to your failure to meet the elements outlined on the growth plan." Ms. Moore immediately burst into tears and responded:

> What? Why? I did a great job. I had an overall good score; I only got Below Expectations in one area. The overall evaluation is good. How can this happen? I messed up a few times, but I learned from it and will not ever curse at a student or talk about a student in a public place again. You told me that you were contacting Human Resources about my growth plan since you never did one before, but you never got back with me about it. I didn't know the growth plan was in effect because you never mentioned it again.

Mrs. Gordon listened as Ms. Moore sobbed, but stated that:

> The district policy states that a person on a probationary contract can be nonrenewed at any time during the first year of employment with that district. And the district policy states that failure to comply with terms on the growth plan can result in an educator not being renewed. We talked about your growth plan after the event. This meeting is over.

Furious and upset with the outcome of the meeting, Ms. Moore left school immediately. She felt that she was unfairly treated and had recourse to file a grievance regarding the decision. Furthermore, Ms. Moore contacted her professional association/union and asked for legal guidance as she questioned the process of filing a grievance. She decided to begin the process of filing a grievance requesting that she keep her job. She noted the following on her grievance report:

> *The purpose of this grievance is to have my performance re-evaluated this year. My overall evaluation from this year is good, yet I am being nonrenewed*

for failure to comply with terms on the growth plan. However, I was never given a growth plan or specific steps to take in order to improve my performance. I understand that I am on a probationary contract and that district policy states that a person on a probationary contract can be nonrenewed during the first year and there is a process for appealing the decision. However, I feel I am getting nonrenewed in an unethical fashion. I never received a growth plan and I had positive marks on all areas except one which were noted on my evaluation as "Below Expectations." I also feel that I was harassed by Mrs. Klein as she made unwarranted comments and complaints against me which didn't help Mrs. Gordon's perception of me.

After filing the grievance Ms. Moore did not hear back from Human Resources or anyone else in central office until the last weeks of the school year. On the last day of school she received her letter of nonrenewal.

THE LITERATURE REVIEW

The case study presented several points of contention regarding Ms. Moore's performance and her contract being nonrenewed. It is important to understand the research related to various issues involving this case study. This section highlights relevant research on the need for beginning teacher supports, effective classroom management skills, code of ethics, and illegal practices.

Beginning Teacher Supports

Decades of research suggest that the teaching profession is a revolving door in which a majority of beginning teachers leave the profession within the first five years (Ingersoll & Smith, 2004; Ingersoll, 2012). Not only are the beginning years of novice teachers demanding, it is emotionally taxing as well (Liston, Whitcomb, & Borko, 2006). While districts and states have adopted mentoring practices to help curb the exit rate of teachers, the rates are still very high. Research supports that induction programs have had a positive impact (Elliott, Issacs, & Chugani, 2010).

The issues first year teachers struggle with the most (classroom management, instructional practices and navigating the political climate) has been curtailed slowly by mentoring and induction programs (Ingersoll, 2012). Classroom management is hard to implement for beginning teachers often because they have never had opportunities to practice it before. They are trained on theoretical structures of best classroom practices, but often do not get to practice these techniques until they are employed the first year of teaching.

As we know, effective classroom management is viewed as a pillar of student learning (Emmer & Stough, 2001). Everston (2001) affirms the importance of classroom management in order to have a successful and productive learning environment. If a teacher does not have a solid grasp of management techniques, then they are not able to effectively control the environment where students are able to engage and learn the content. Furthermore, classroom management problems are the main reasons that lead to burnout and novice teachers leaving the profession (Everston & Weinstein, 2006).

Additionally, classroom management is imperative for teachers teaching adolescents who have dwindling motivation (Beaty-O'Ferrall, Green & Hanna, 2010). Evertson, Emmer, and Worsham (2003) identified important components of classroom management, including beginning the school year with a positive emphasis on management; arranging the room in a way conducive to effective management; and identifying and implementing rules and operating procedures.

Furthermore, it is important that beginning teachers are equipped with knowledge and skills about how to implement effective management practices. Many times in dealing with troubled students behavioral issues, teachers' emotions take over and they may take part in a fight or flight response. Often this fight response is triggered by emotional response that beginning teachers do not have practice or understanding in how to handle; therefore, they engage in unprofessional acts that they would not normally do if given time to stop, think and apply beforehand. With this Liston, Whitcomb, and Borko (2006) suggest that teacher education programs need to "do a better job preparing candidates for the emotional intensity that awaits them in their first years."

Ethical Practices

The profession of teaching is held to a high caliber of ethical conduct. Since teachers interact with young children on a daily basis, it is important that they uphold high levels of professional practice. Developing and following a professional code of ethics helps make sure teachers act in a professional and ethical manner at all times.

It is essential that all educators, not just teachers, in a school uphold ethical principles as well. Many states have employed specific teacher code of ethics as well as administrator and principal code of ethics. It is important that administrators uphold ethical practices to not only students, but the faculty and staff on their campus. Similar to legal ramifications related to unethical practices of teachers being disciplined or removing their credentials, administrators must uphold ethical practices that promote autonomy and leadership on the campus. If they fail to uphold ethical standards and due diligence, then they can also face legal implications.

THE GUIDING QUESTIONS

The following questions are posed to assist in addressing issues of ethical conduct in the case study. While an example of school district policies and state codes are provided in the literature review, use your own state policies to address the questions.

1. Nothing is mentioned in the case about Ms. Moore having a mentor teacher. The only mention of guidance for her first year was through consultation with her team. Could a mentor teacher have been of assistance in this situation? Could having a mentor potentially prevented Ms. Moore from using vulgar language to the student?

    - Could there be legal implications for failing to have an assigned mentor teacher to a first year teacher?

2. Was it acceptable for Ms. Moore and her team to review Greg's permanent file? Could any discipline issues with Greg have been prevented if further action was taken regarding his past use of profanity?
3. Even though Ms. Moore established early lines of communication with Greg's parents before the event, the mom was demanding at the conference that she been reprimanded for her behavior. Was it ethical for Mrs. Gordon to respond to the parent that Ms. Moore was being reprimanded for her use of profanity with Greg?
4. Was it ethical for Mrs. Klein to report the incident to the principal in the first place? Should Mrs. Klein have had a conversation with Ms. Moore before reporting the incident to the principal?
5. Was it necessary that Mrs. Klein be in the meeting regarding the event with Ms. Selman and Mrs. Gordon; Was it ethical to discuss Ms. Moore's situation in a meeting with another teacher present? Was it ethical for Ms. Moore to be reprimanded in front of Mrs. Klein?
6. Was Ms. Moore justified in sending Greg to the office once he verbally insulted her in the class?
7. Was it justified for Ms. Moore to be reprimanded for speaking about the situation and using Greg's name during happy hour with her non-teacher friends?
8. What ethical and legal implications could Ms. Moore face other than reprimand for using vulgar language at a student?
9. Mrs. Gordon mentioned that Mrs. Klein (who is in her Sunday school class) told her about Ms. Moore sharing details of the week (including personal information about a child) out in a public place? What does policy or ethics say about sharing information about a student for non-educational purposes?

10. Mrs. Gordon noted that Ms. Moore would have two documented instances on her performance evaluation and would need to be on a growth plan; however, she never gets back with Ms. Moore about specific steps on her growth plan. Does Ms. Moore have legal recourse to appeal the decision of a nonrenewable contract?
11. As an administrator, how might you handle the situation differently? Detail all the elements in the case that are unethical/illegal and your process for handling the many issues in the case.

FINAL CONSIDERATIONS

The case study mentioned in this chapter involves several problems that could have been avoided if proper channels were followed and if specific protocols were in place. Some of the ways the issues in the case could have been prevented:

1. Not discussing student personal information and behaviors with others (unless used for educational reasons) is a violation of the Code of Ethics and State Law per this case. What does your school district policy and state law say?
2. There was not a need for Mrs. Klein (art teacher) to be present in the meeting with Mr. Selman, Mrs. Gordon, and Ms. Moore. Ms. Moore was reprimanded in front of a colleague, which had negative implications and was unprofessional. What is your school district policy for filing a grievance or reporting information in which a teacher feels violates ethical conduct?
3. Not under any circumstance should Ms. Moore curse at a student. This is a violation of the Educator Code of Ethics. Does your school policy or educator code of ethics give specific examples of unethical and unprofessional conduct?
4. Mrs. Gordon is also bound to the Educator Code of Ethics; therefore, she should not have shared that Ms. Moore had been "reprimanded" with a parent. What is the route Ms. Moore should have taken according to your district policy?
5. Ms. Moore could have reported the incident to the parent immediately. She also could have informed the administrators of the incident. Does your school policy have a specific chain of command for reporting incidents in which a teacher feels they made a mistake?
6. Ms. Moore did not have an assigned mentor teacher. There are several implications this had on the (un)ethical practices of the administration. What is your district policy and state policy regarding beginning teachers being assigned a mentor teacher?

7. Ms. Moore was informed of a growth plan verbally, but never received documentation of the plan or what she was to do to improve. This has implications on the legality of her termination. What is your school district and state policy regarding beginning teacher's employment clause? Does a beginning teacher have opportunities to file a grievance for unethical practices with the district and/or the state?

REFERENCES

Darling-Hammond, L. (2006). *Powerful teacher education: Lessons from exemplary programs.* San Francisco: Jossey-Bass.

Elliott, E., Issacs, M., & Chugani, C. (2010). Promoting self-efficacy in early career teachers: A principal's guide to differentiated mentoring and supervision. *Florida Journal Education Administration and Policy, (4)*1, 131-146.

Emmer, E., & Stough, L. (2001). Classroom management: A crucial part of educational psychology, with implications for teacher education. *Educational Psychologist, 36*(2), 103-112.

Evertson, C. M., & Weinstein, C. S. (2006). Classroom management as a field of inquiry, Handbook of classroom management: *Research, Practice and Contemporary Issues*. Mahwah, NJ: Lawrence Erlbaum Associations.

Evertson, C. M., Emmer, E . T., & Worsham, M. E. (2003). *Classroom management for elementary teachers* (6th Edition). Boston: Allyn and Bacon.

Greenfield, W. D. (1991). *Rationale and methods to articulate ethics and administrator training.* Paper presented at the annual meeting of the American Educational Research Association, Chicago, April 1991. Retrieved from http://files.eric.ed.gov/fulltext/ED332379.pdf

Ingersoll, R. M. (2012). Beginning teacher induction: What the data tell us. *Phi Delta Kappan, 93*(8), 47-51.

Ingersoll, R. M., & Smith, T. M. (2004). Do teacher induction and mentoring matter? *NASSP Bulletin, 88*(638), 28-40.

Liston, D., Whitcomb, J., & Borko, H. (2006). Too little or too much: Teacher preparation and the first years of teaching. *Journal of Teacher Education, 57*(4), 351-358.

Beaty-O'Ferrall, M., Green, A., & Hanna, F. (2010). Classroom management strategies for difficult students: Promoting change through relationships. *Middle School Journal, 41*, 4-11.

Chapter Two

Investigating the Demands and Challenges of Critical Thinking Instruction

Gina Anderson and Jody Piro

The importance of critical thinking as a necessary skill to prepare students for college and the workforce is well-documented. The Program for International Student Assessment (PISA) and Trends in International Mathematics and Science Study (TIMMS) require students to demonstrate critical thinking, and the Common Core State Standards indicate critical thinking is an interdisciplinary skill that is crucial for success in schools (Wardlow, 2014). Finally, Forbes magazine listed critical thinking as number one from the ten most critical job skills in 2013 (Casserly, 2012).

Despite these directives, critical thinking instruction has many challenges. How is critical thinking defined? What does it look like? How can it be assessed? The following case demonstrates some of the complex issues surrounding critical thinking and its implementation in the classroom. Following the case, the authors provide several critical thinking instructional strategies for developing critical thinking in instructional contexts. Last, questions guide the reader into a deeper analysis of some of the topics that may emerge from using each of the critical thinking instructional strategies in classrooms.

THE CASE STUDY

Back to School

Typically, the first week of school at Hollyhill High School is considered an exciting one. The kickoff of a new school year usually brings about a feeling of starting fresh with new students, new classes, and new opportunities. This year the football team, as well as several other sports and extracurricular groups, are expected to soar and make it to state play-offs or other statewide competitions.

The principal, Mr. Ferris, is in his 3rd year at the school, and he and his assistant principals have worked hard to create and sustain a culture that nurtures faculty development and student success in the areas of academics, athletics, leadership, and global citizenship. Student test scores were going up and misconduct issues were going down. School spirit was at an all-time high. Teacher turn-over was at an all-time low. It has been a great time to be a Hollyhill Heatwave!

This year at Hollyhill started off quite differently. It was the first week of classes, and the hallways were full of tension. School rankings were just made public, and Hollyhill High School's accountability rating went down. Teachers, parents, and students were worried about the consequences. An emergency faculty meeting was called after school on Friday, and faculty and staff were nervous. Were certain teachers going to lose their jobs or be reassigned? What other mandates or high-stakes decisions would be made?

The Faculty Meeting

"Greetings, colleagues," began Mr. Ferris. "I regret the need to call an emergency meeting on a Friday." You could hear a pin drop in the room. "I first want to remind you how much I appreciate all of the hard work and dedication you put forth for our school. It takes all of us working together and doing our part to keep our school running in a positive manner. We have celebrated many successes over these last few years, and I know we will continue to encounter many more together."

He paused, and the faculty and staff looked at each other, waiting for the other shoe to drop. "Despite our many successes, we have recently been notified of areas of improvement, and as you know, our accountability ranking went down. Our standardized test scores were analyzed not only in regard to our state standards but were also disaggregated, for the first time, according to any standards requiring critical thinking. Hollyhill students scored significantly lower on critical thinking standards when compared to our sister high schools in the district as well as all other public high schools across the state. These results naturally have our School Board concerned, and we will have to work strategically and quickly to improve these scores. Therefore, I have decided, in cooperation with all of the content area curriculum specialists, that we will focus all of our professional development on critical thinking instruction this year."

Faculty Response

The faculty members were shocked at these results. After all, Hollyhill High School has the distinctive honor of serving as one of the Global Diploma schools in the district. This distinction was earned after a rigorous application and review process of the school's curriculum and pedagogical practices. Global Diploma schools have a reputation for high standards and for preparing students for success in a rapidly changing, global society. An approved, international curriculum must be utilized, and critical thinking instruction was embedded across the diploma program.

Mr. Alford, one of the U.S. history teachers, called Mrs. Murray, the Advanced Placement English teacher. "Can you believe what we heard today? What do you think about this?"

Mrs. Murray said, "No, this was such unexpected news. Within the English curriculum the students read diverse literature and use many higher order thinking skills to demonstrate understanding of all of the reading elements. I thought we were doing just fine in this area!"

Mr. Alford replied, "I know what you mean. In my class, for example, we discuss multiple perspectives of Westward Expansion and then the students write a critique of O'Sullivan's *Manifest Destiny*. Aren't we helping our students develop critical thinking skills with these approaches?"

Mr. Ramón, the physics teacher, felt quite differently than his English and U.S. history colleagues regarding the mandate to increase critical thinking. He grumbled to himself, "Well, here we go again. I thought this issue was settled a couple of years ago when our state politicians opposed higher order thinking skills and critical thinking because of their focus on behavior modification. It isn't our place to challenge students' fixed beliefs and undermine their parent's authority! Let's just stick to curriculum that is objective and factual! My science curriculum is pretty black and white, so I don't need to mess with this critical thinking stuff."

The Challenges Begin

Soon, the teachers and curriculum specialists began meeting and attending professional development workshops. Questions were asked, such as how is critical thinking defined? How do we know what it looks like? What is the best way to teach it? How can we assess it? How can we respond to any parents who may object?

Teachers were finding it difficult to settle upon a common definition of critical thinking. At the end of a brainstorming session, it was finally agreed upon that questioning was a common element in critical thinking. Questions that elicited more information, probed deeper, and sought out different perspectives seemed to be key. Next, one of the curriculum specialists asked,

"So, now that we have an idea of how critical thinking is defined, how do we teach it? Please share with your partner a way that you think you teach critical thinking in your subject area."

Mrs. Murray turned to Mr. Alford. She considered him for a few seconds, and then said, "Well, to be honest, I ask a lot of open-ended questions and provide many opportunities for students to discuss their perspectives. Isn't that an example of critical thinking?"

Mr. Alford replied, "What do you do when a student responds in a way that is informed more by opinion than support from the text? Or, what if a student overlooks another important perspective to be considered?"

"Oh, well sometimes the students work those things out between themselves. If not, then sometimes I follow-up with more direct instruction the next day," said Mrs. Murray.

"But does that help them develop better critical thinking skills? Or, does that simply inform them about what you want them to learn?" countered Mr. Alford.

Mrs. Fujimoto, the Geometry teacher, overheard Mr. Alford's and Mrs. Murray's discussion. "You know, when I am teaching a complex formula, I have to break it down into separate parts, first. I also need to provide a benchmark of the steps required in that formula to master so that the students do not get too overwhelmed. Then, we stop and 'think about our thinking' and either share out loud or in a journal those thoughts before moving on. I wonder if a similar kind of approach could be used in your literature and U.S. history discussions."

Mr. Ramón chimed in. "Well, in physics it would be a waste of time to stop and 'think about our thinking.' The laws of gravity are not exactly discussion material. Who can argue with Newton?"

"But wait!" said Mrs. Murray. "Isn't Newton's work a theory? Can't theories be disproven? New evidence and insights about science are discovered all the time! Wouldn't it be amazing if one of your students discovered something new about gravity?"

The curriculum specialist called the attention back up to the front and said, "After listening to your conversations with your colleagues, I can tell that some new insights about critical thinking instruction are emerging! One of these ideas is that critical thinking does not just happen on its own. Just because we provide an opportunity to read and discuss something compelling doesn't mean that critical thought will result. Furthermore, other areas of academics that we may take for granted as determined, factual, or objective are actually debatable and have much room for further investigation. It might be helpful to know that research actually supports these ideas!"

The curriculum specialist continued, "Critical thinking is more likely to occur when instruction is scaffolded and frameworks are used. In fact, a framework not only helps us model critical thinking, scaffold the instruction of it, help our students and us recognize it when it happens, but also helps us assess it."

"Well, I hate to be the squeaky wheel, but we are all forgetting something," Mr. Ramón retorted. "For the most part, we serve a very conservative community, and many of our kids have parents with very clear beliefs and attitudes about certain topics. What if they go home talking about the debate between the theory of evolution and the idea of intelligent design? Or, what if one of these so-called critical thinking discussions leads to a change in their political or religious perspectives? What then? How will we handle those complaints?"

Mr. Ferris, the principal, just happened to walk by at that time to check to see how the professional development session was going. "I can take care of any complaints. You just keep working hard. I'll remind the parents that not only are their kids a member of their family but also a member of a community, state, nation, and global society. We don't tell them what to think, but instead help them to think for themselves. To thrive in a democratic, global society our students need to not only navigate their personal beliefs and traditions but also the many others that are present in our diverse world. While critical thinking is sure to provide some discomfort, this is a necessary step in the learning process."

THE LITERATURE REVIEW

The above case demonstrates some of the challenges and demands associated with critical thinking instruction and assessment within a modern school setting. This is reflected in the questions with which the teachers grappled, such as how is critical thinking defined? How do we know what it looks like? What is the best way to teach it? How can we assess it? The following sections develop perspectives on defining and teaching critical thinking by scaffolding instruction and applying a framework within discussions. Additionally, assessment strategies and other resources are shared.

What Is Critical Thinking?

Critical thinking is difficult to define, but philosophers, psychologists, and educators alike tend to agree that questions eliciting deeper thought within discussions are an essential defining characteristic (Lai, 2011; Paul, Martin, & Adamson, 1989). More specifically, Socratic questioning within discussions is a systematic approach to facilitate critical thinking (Golding, 2011; Knezic et al., 2010; Paul & Elder, 2007).

Socratic questions may be used strategically in discussions to examine points of view and gain new insights. Socratic questions may stimulate thought, define tasks, express problems, identify assumptions, explore multiple perspectives, and often generate further questions in order to continue thought and analysis (Elder & Paul, 2008). A change in values or beliefs is not necessarily an outcome of critical thinking via Socratic questioning; however, these processes may serve to further inform perspectives and one's ability to engage in civil discourse within a democratic society (Anderson & Piro, 2015, 2014a, 2013; Piro & Anderson, 2015, 2016; Phillips, 2001; Siegel, 1988).

Can Critical Thinking be Taught?

The development of critical thinking skills is often an ambiguous practice (Banks, 2008; Elder, 2004; Gay & Howard, 2000) and rarely occurs without instructional scaffolding of some kind (Abrami et al., 2008; Facione, 1990; Halpern, 1998; Hew & Cheung, 2003; Landsman & Gorski, 2007; Paul, 1992). The use of frameworks within discussions may help scaffold instruction, identify and benchmark Socratic questions that are applied, and therefore increase the probability and occurrence of critical thinking (Piro & Anderson, 2015; Halpern, 1998). Discussion without a framework, or a framework used in isolation, may increase the ambiguity and challenges of teaching critical thinking skills.

Christopher Phillips (2001) is credited with a discussion approach known as Socrates Café. Phillips facilitated his Socrates Cafe discussion groups in coffee shops, libraries, schools, and other public spaces in order to engage more voices in democratic discourse over complex topics. According to Phillips (2001, p. 20) Socrates Café "reveals people to themselves" and "makes them see what their opinions really amount to..." and "...is not so much a search for absolute truth and certainty as it is a quest for honesty" (Phillips, 2001, p. 53). Socrates Café formats can be simulated in face-to-face classrooms, online settings, and cooperative groups by creating a safe community for Socratic questions and discussion.

Metacognition is commonly known as awareness or analysis of one's own learning or thinking and is an idea that can be traced back to Socrates's questioning methods (Tanner, 2012). Furthermore, metacognition is integral to the critical thinking process (Kuhn, 1999; Lai, 2011; Magno, 2010). Elder and Paul (2008) identify three levels of thought that shape human thinking.

The first level of thinking is primarily unreflective and self-serving; the second level of thinking is selectively reflective and lacks critical thinking, and the third level of thinking is explicitly reflective and regularly includes critical thinking tools in analyzing and assessing thinking (p. 7). In order to help foster metacognition and level three thinking skills, Elder and Paul (2008) developed the Universal Intellectual Standards. These standards utilize questions that are Socratic in nature to improve the quality of thinking.

Elder and Paul's (2008) Universal Intellectual Standards include clarity, accuracy, precision, relevance, depth, breadth, logic, significance, and fairness of expression. They suggest the following questions to demonstrate each standard:

1. Clarity: Could you elaborate further? Could you give me an example? Could you illustrate what you mean?
2. Accuracy: How could we check on that? How could we find out if that is true? How could we verify or test that?
3. Precision: Could you be more specific? Could you give me more details? Could you be more exact?
4. Relevance: How does that relate to the problem? How does that bear on the question? How does that help us with the issue?
5. Depth: What factors make this a difficult problem? What are some of the complexities of this question? What are some of the difficulties we need to deal with?
6. Breadth: Do we need to look at this from another perspective? Do we need to consider another point of view? Do we need to look at this in other ways?
7. Logic: Does all this make sense together? Does your first paragraph fit in with your last? Does what you say follow from the evidence?
8. Significance: Is this the most important problem to consider? Is this the central idea to focus on? Which of these facts are most important?
9. Fairness: Do I (you, they, etc.) have any vested interest in this issue? Am I (you, they, etc.) sympathetically representing the viewpoints of others? (p. 5)

The questions exemplifying each of the standards are Socratic in nature, help students investigate unexamined assumptions and viewpoints, and facilitate the development of new insights. Discussion protocols utilizing a simulated Socrates Café approach and the Universal Intellectual Standards in tandem have been adapted for a variety of educational settings; K-12 and higher education instruction, face-to-face and online classrooms, and jigsaw cooperative groups and have shown promise in the development of students' critical thinking skills (Anderson & Piro, 2015, 2014a, 2013; Piro & Anderson, 2015, 2016). An at-a-glance Universal Intellectual Standards Quick Reference Guide is provided in Appendix B.

Implementation and Assessment of Critical Thinking

There are several ways to implement and assess critical thinking instruction, but for the purposes of this case, a general discussion protocol, a jigsaw cooperative group approach, and a self-assessment will be emphasized. All three strategies utilize Socratic Questioning and the Universal Intellectual Standards as a framework for scaffolding critical thinking instruction and assessment.

General Discussion Protocol

The General Discussion Protocol was created by the authors of this case study chapter and complements the Universal Intellectual Standards as a framework to scaffold critical thinking instruction. This protocol can be used in tandem with the adaptations of Socrates Café for K-12, higher education, face-to-face, online, and self-assessments.

There are three steps to the Discussion Protocol: 1) read (or listen), 2) reflect, and 3) respond. The first step helps students focus on the problem or issue. Step two provides an opportunity for students to apply metacognition and prepare for discussion and dialogue. Step three includes the intellectual standards as a guiding reference as students participate in the discussion in a respectful manner. A copy of the full protocol may be found in Appendix A.

Jigsaw Cooperative Group Approach

A Jigsaw cooperative group approach to critical thinking instruction is implemented by following a series of seven steps. These steps are modified from both Socrates Café (Phillips, 2001) and Jigsaw cooperative grouping concepts (Aronson, 2017; Aronson & Patnoe, 2011). The authors of this case study fashioned the following steps for what they termed a Jigsaw Socrates Café (Anderson & Piro, 2014a, 2013).

The Jigsaw Socrates Café steps demonstrate scaffolded instruction within a cooperative group activity and include a graphic organizer for recording questions. See Appendix C for a full description and graphic of the seven steps as well as a copy of the graphic organizer.

Self-Assessment

Following a discussion, students may gauge their own use of dialogue or discussion, Socratic questioning, intellectual standards, scholarliness, interactions and dispositions within the discussion. Subsequently, they may devise a growth plan for each element for succeeding Socrates Cafés. As they exit the class, the self-assessment can be submitted anonymously or identified, depending on the teachers' instructional goals. Table 2.2 in Appendix C demonstrates a sample self-assessment exit ticket.

THE GUIDING QUESTIONS

Respond to the following questions about the case using the Universal Intellectual Standards. Hint: Consider responding with additional questions that probe the issues deeper or that elicit new perspectives or insights. Consider gauging the type of intellectual standard you use with your questions.

1. Mrs. Murray expressed the notion that exposure to diverse texts was an example of critical thinking. If you had the chance to talk to Mrs. Murray, how might you continue the conversation? What could you say to her that might further prompt her to investigate her perspectives of critical thinking instruction?
2. Mr. Alford's students appear to write critiques of historical practices and documents. What questions might help confirm whether this pedagogical approach is eliciting evidence of critical thinking from his students?
3. What is the relationship between open-ended questions and Socratic questions? Is there a difference between the two? Explain.
4. Mr. Alford queries Mrs. Murray's use of open-ended questions and discussions by asking, "What do you do when a student responds in a way that is informed more by opinion than support from the text? Or, what if a student overlooks another important perspective to be considered? Which of the nine intellectual standards might represent his questions (there may be more than one standard that applies)? What is the value of asking students to ground their opinions in common readings?
5. When would Mrs. Murray use a General Discussion Protocol? A Jigsaw Discussion? Are there certain topics that are best used in one or the other forms of discussion? Are there certain instructional goals that would guide the use of one or the other form of discussion, such as time constraints or hoping that typically quiet students would be able to become more engaged in discussions?
6. Instead of direct instruction, how might Mrs. Murray guide her students to consider different perspectives and to support them with examples from a text or research? How might she implement and assess this instruction?
7. Mr. Alford questioned Mrs. Murray's use of direct instruction to develop her students' critical thinking skills by asking, "[But] does that help them develop better critical thinking skills? Or, does that simply inform them about what you want them to learn?" What additional questions could Mr. Alford ask? Which of the intellectual standards do they represent?

8. Mrs. Fujimoto describes a process she follows when she teaches a complex Geometry formula. This is known as scaffolded instruction. How are the frameworks offered by the authors' examples of scaffolding for critical thinking? How might scaffolding critical thinking help students produce Socratic questioning?
9. Mr. Ramón was concerned that his curriculum was not conducive to critical thinking instruction as the other teachers planned to use it. How might Mrs. Murray help Mr. Ramón use the intellectual standards in his curriculum?
10. Mr. Ferris and many other principals and teachers across our nation's schools work with colleagues like Mr. Ramón, who are not enthusiastic about developing critical thinking into his existing curriculum. They must also act with diplomacy with parents and other community members who may not always agree with school practices. Complex issues and challenging conversations are the "norm" for educators. Which of the intellectual standards might apply to issues of diplomacy, democracy, and civil discourse?
11. How might student self-assessment of Socratic questioning within discussions promote critical thinking in your classroom?
12. The critical thinking strategies presented in this case study can be adapted for a variety of settings. What is one new approach you could easily implement into your own critical thinking instruction and assessment practices? Is there a strategy that seems less applicable to your class or more difficult to implement? Why?

FINAL CONSIDERATIONS

While considering possible responses to the questions above, maintain awareness of the thinking that is occurring. Does it appear to be unreflective and self-serving? Is it selectively reflective in some situations but not in others? How many of the different types of intellectual standards are being used? Responses to the guiding questions may take the form of additional questions, primarily Socratic in nature, and typically do not have a clear cut answer. Possible responses to the guiding questions follow below.

1. Ask Mrs. Murray to elaborate further or provide examples of the diverse texts and assessments used that measure higher order thinking/critical thinking (clarity). What counts as a diverse text? Does exposure to diverse texts guarantee critical thinking? How can she be sure (accuracy)? Do the diverse texts truly represent multiple voices, ethnicities, genders, worldviews, etc.? Do the texts include biased perspectives? If so, are the biases identified and discussed in order to

elicit higher order thinking/critical thinking? What are some of the difficulties [of text selection, higher order thinking skills, critical thinking] that we need to deal with (depth)?
2. Ask Mr. Alford to discuss the format of the assignment as well as his assessment measure. How does he define "critique" (clarity)? Does he use a framework for scaffolding the skill of critiquing? Ask for details (precision). Mr. Alford stated that his students discuss multiple perspectives of the themes of the book. How are the multiple perspectives elicited in a way that represents the viewpoints of others (fairness)? What other methods are used to critique literature? All of the intellectual standards could be applied when writing a critique.
3. Typically, both Socratic and open-ended questions do not have determined, clear-cut answers. However, Socratic questions are more deliberative and strategic in the goal of probing the deeper, more complex elements of a dilemma or issue. Socratic questioning may disrupt unexamined, pre-existing attitudes and can bring about change or the broadening of one's viewpoints. Open-ended questions do not necessarily require levels of deep thinking and the examining of personal attitudes and viewpoints.
4. What do you do when a student responds in a way that is informed more by opinion than support from the text (clarity; precision)? What if a student overlooks another important perspective to be considered (breadth; fairness)? The value of asking students to ground their opinions in common readings facilitates their critical thinking in a number of ways. First, it helps them become aware that their opinion is only one perspective to be considered. Two, it helps them examine whether their opinion may be rooted in emotion or personal beliefs rather than research, data, trends, etc. Three, it provides context and common ground between and among all participants in the discussion; thus enhancing the discussion and participation in democratic, civil discourse.
5. Mrs. Murray could use a General Discussion Protocol as a framework for discussion and critical thinking instruction. The General Discussion Protocol is especially helpful when first introducing the intellectual standards as well as when using them to help scaffold and assess critical thinking. The Jigsaw Discussion could be considered for small group discussions when time is not limited and when rapport-building is a goal. Complex issues that are typically considered dilemmas rather than problems in need of a solution are good discussion topics. Reserved or quiet students tend to be more engaged in a Jigsaw Discussion rather than a large group discussion. Student self-assessments of discussions may also be effective in engaging students in metacognition and reflection of their critical thinking discussions.

6. The General Discussion Protocol, Jigsaw Discussion, and Self-Assessments utilizing the intellectual standards may be considered indirect approaches that help students consider different perspectives that are grounded with examples from texts or research. Direct instruction may be used to teach the protocol, the jigsaw, and the intellectual standards. Modeling and guided practice are integral to the successful implementation. Two assessment resources, the Self-Assessment Graphic Organizer and Exit Ticket are provided in the appendices.
7. [But] does that help them develop better critical thinking skills (accuracy)? Or, does that simply inform them about what you want them to learn (precision)? Does direct instruction of critical thinking make sense together (logic)? How could direct instruction relate to the problem (relevance)? How might it limit the development of other perspectives or points of view (breadth)?
8. The intellectual standards framework as well as the discussion methods provided in this chapter may provide a foundation and incremental steps for the instruction, practice, and assessment of critical thinking. Critical thinking by way of Socratic questioning is a skill that can be developed, and it is less likely to occur without scaffolded instruction.
9. Mrs. Murray might start by using the intellectual standards herself in a respectful discussion with Mr. Ramón. She might ask questions like: "How can we find out if a certain scientific theory is true (accuracy)? Do you ask your students to verify or test their hypotheses (accuracy)? Does what they say follow from the evidence (logic)? Which facts from the evidence are the most important (significance)? Do you ask your students to consider the "gray" in addition to the "black and white" (depth)? Are there ethical issues and other viewpoints to consider (fairness)?"
10. Many, if not all, of the intellectual standards apply to issues of diplomacy, democracy, and civil discourse and may help support difficult discussions. Since the intellectual standards are primarily demonstrated with Socratic questions, it allows for the dialogue to continue in a respectful way. The intellectual standards relevance, depth, breadth, significance, and fairness are especially articulated in ways that elicit metacognition, reflection, and critical analysis of matters that go beyond the self and therefore apply to issues of diplomacy, democracy, and civil discourse.
11. Self-assessment of Socratic questioning that is framed and benchmarked by the intellectual standards helps students gain more awareness and gauge their own progress of critical analysis. Scholarliness, interactions, and dispositions within the discussion may also be examined during the self-assessment. Enhanced awareness may lead to increased metacognition, reflection, and stronger critical thinking skills.

12. Responses will vary. Consider implementing a critical thinking strategy that will be simple to carry out and that will complement existing curriculum and instruction.

REFERENCES

Abrami, P. C., Bernard, R., Borokhovski, E., Wade, A., Surkes, M., Tamim, R., & Zhang, Dai. (2008). Instructional interventions affecting critical thinking skills and dispositions: A stage 1 meta-analysis. *Review of Educational Research, 78*(4), 1102–1134.

Anderson, G., & Piro, J. (2015). Developing teacher dispositions in Socrates Café: Implications for English language learners. In Cowart, M.T. and Anderson, G. (Eds.) *Professional Practice in Diverse Settings: Attitudes and Dispositions That Facilitate Success*. Arlington, VA: Canh Nam Publishers, Inc.

Anderson, G., & Piro, J. (2014a). Jigsaw Socrates Café for diversity and social justice. *Encyclopedia of Diversity and Social Justice Project*. Lanham, MD: Rowman & Littlefield.

Anderson, G., & Piro, J. (2014b). Conversations in Socrates Café: Scaffolding critical thinking via Socratic questioning and dialogues. *New Horizons for Learning, 11*(1), 1-9.

Anderson, G., & Piro, J. (2013, Fall). The Socrates café is now open: Scaffolding critical analysis within a cooperative activity. In Cowart, M.T. and Anderson, G. (Eds.) *Teaching and Leading in Diverse Schools*. Arlington, VA: Canh Nam Publishers, Inc.

Aronson, E. (2017). The jigsaw classroom. Retrieved from https://www.jigsaw.org/.

Aronson, E., & Patnoe, S. (2011). *Cooperation in the classroom: The jigsaw method* (3rd Edition). London, UK: Pinter & Martin.

Banks, J. A. (2008). *An introduction to multicultural education* (4th ed.). Boston: Pearson.

Casserly, M. (2012, December 10). *The 10 skills that will get you hired in 2013*. Forbes. Retrieved from http://www.forbes.com/sites/meghancasserly/2012/12/10/the-10-skillsthat-will-get-you-a-job-in-2013/.

Elder, L. (2004, Winter). Diversity: Making sense of it through critical thinking. *Journal for Quality & Participation, 27*(4), 9-13.

Elder, L., & Paul, R. (2008). *Intellectual standards: The words that name them and the criteria that define them*. Dillon Beach, CA: Foundation for Critical Thinking.

Facione, P. A. (1990). *Critical thinking: A statement of expert consensus for purposes of educational assessment and instruction*. Millbrae, CA: The California Academic Press.

Gay, G., & Howard, T. (2000). Multicultural teacher education for the 21st century. *The Teacher Educator, 36*(1), 1-16.

Golding, C. (2011). Educating for critical thinking: Thought-encouraging questions in a community of inquiry. *Higher Education Research & Development, 30*(3), 357-370.

Halpern, D. (1998). Teaching critical thinking for transfer across domains: Dispositions, skills, structure training, and metacognitive monitoring. *American Psychologist, 53*(4), 449–455.

Hew, K., & Cheung, W. (2003). Evaluating the participation and quality of thinking of preservice teachers in an asynchronous online discussion environment: Part II. *International Journal of Instructional Media, 30*(4), 173-186.

Knezic, D., Wubbels, T., Elbers, E., & Hajer, M. (2010). The Socratic dialogue and teacher education. *Teaching and Teacher Education, 26*(4), 1104-1111.

Kuhn, D. (1999). A developmental model of critical thinking. *Educational Researcher, 28*(2), 16-46.

Lai, E. (2011). Critical thinking: A literature review. *Pearson's Research Reports, 6*, 1-49.

Landsman, J., & Gorski, P. (2007). Countering standardization. *Educational Leadership, 64*(8), 40–41.

Magno, C. (2010). The role of metacognitive skills in developing critical thinking. *Metacognition Learning, 5*(2), 137-156. DOI: 10.1007/s11409-010-9054-4.

McCarthy, E. (2008). Comparative philosophy and the liberal arts: Between and beyond – educating to cultivate geocitizens. *Canadian Review of American Studies, 38*(2), 293-309.

Paul, R. (1992). Critical thinking: What, why, and how? *New Directions for Community Colleges, 1992*(77), 3-24.

Paul, R., & Elder, L. (2007). Critical thinking: The art of Socratic questioning. *Journal of Developmental Education, 31*(1), 34-37.

Paul, R., Martin, D., & Adamson, K. (1989). *Critical thinking handbook: High school*. Dillon Beach, CA: Foundation for Critical Thinking.

Phillips, C. (2001). *Socrates café: A fresh taste of philosophy*. New York, NY: Norton.

Piro, J., & Anderson, G. (2016). A typology for an online Socrates café. *Teachers College Record. 118*(7). Retrieved from http://www.tcrecord.org/Content.asp?ContentId=19365.

Piro, J., & Anderson, G. (2015). Discussions in a Socrates café: Implications for critical thinking in teacher education. *Action in Teacher Education, 37*(2), 1-19. DOI: 10.1080/01626620.2015.1048009.

Siegel, H. (1988). *Educating reason: rationality, critical thinking, and education* (Vol. 1). New York: Routledge.

Tanner, K.D. (2012). Promoting student metacognition. *CBE Life Sciences Education, 11*(2), 113-120. DOI: 10.1187/cbe.12-03-0033.

Wardlow, L. (2014). The challenges of teaching critical thinking. *Pearson Research and Innovation Network*. Retrieved from http://researchnetwork.pearson.com/elearning/challenges-teaching-critical-thinking.

Chapter Three

Academic Support and Motivation during Second Language Acquisition

Serious Considerations for Educators

Melinda T. Cowart and Savanna Doroodchi

Each year the number of newcomer English language learners (ELLs) attending U.S. public schools increases dramatically. As of 2013 there were 25.1 million Limited English Proficient (LEP) persons ages 5 and older in the United States, constituting more than 8% of the total population, who resided in the country. Spanish speakers made up 64% (16.2 million) of the total LEP population. Chinese, including Mandarin and Cantonese (1.7 million, or 7%) and Vietnamese (835,000, or 3%) were the next languages most frequently spoken by linguistically diverse individuals (Zong & Batilova, 2015). Primary factors leading to continued expansive growth in the numbers of ELLs include immigration, both legal and undocumented, refugee resettlement, political asylum, and a sizable increase in unaccompanied alien children (UACs) crossing into the United States unaccompanied by parents or guardians.

How do the statistics of the various groups of newcomer ELLs combine to make a significant impact on classrooms? The Immigration and Naturalization Act (INA) annually allows up to 675,000 permanent residents to enter the U.S. as immigrants (Immigration Policy Center, n.d.). Approximately 12 million foreign born persons who were living in the United States in 2013 arrived between 2000 and 2009, and another 4.1 million have entered since 2010 (Zong & Batilova, 2015).

During 2013, 69,926 refugees were resettled in the United States. The most common native countries represented among refugees were Iraq, Burma, and Bhutan (Martin & Yankay, 2014). The limit of refugees to be resettled in that fiscal year was 70,000. The ceiling for numbers of refugees to be resettled is a number annually decided upon by the president, in collaboration with Congress.

There is no limit in the number of persons who may be granted political asylum (Immigration Policy Center, n.d.). In 2013, asylum was awarded to 25,199 individuals by the U.S. government (Martin & Yankay, 2014). UACs flee their homelands in search of safe haven following a path that is comparable to that of an asylee rather than a refugee in that they arrive on U.S. soil and petition for asylum from within the United States rather than crossing an international border into the first friendly neighboring country, known as a country of first asylum, to await resettlement. More than 68,500 UACs were detained by the U.S. Customs and Border Patrol in 2014 after being apprehended by authorities in the United States (Meyer et al., 2015).

Thus, the composite of immigration, refugee resettlement and asylum contributes to a vast diversity of peoples, languages, and cultures. In the North Central Texas area alone, at least 239 different languages are spoken as various first languages accompanied by 239 different cultures (Weiss-Armush, 2010). Many of the speakers of the various languages will enroll their children in public schools with the expectation that they will be taught by knowledgeable teachers who are cognizant of their linguistically diverse students' needs and most critical concerns regarding education and academic success (Cowart, 2012).

A recently conducted interview of a twenty-six-year-old Hispanic male, who emigrated from Mexico to the United States as a child and spent a substantial amount of time in the public school system, revealed various aspects of his language acquisition process. The information provided by this informant, along with a perusal of related literature, pointed to further examination of the importance of culturally responsive teaching (CRT) and parental involvement as significant factors in promoting the academic achievement of ELLs. His story is told through the case study that follows.

THE CASE STUDY

In an interview conducted with Diego Hernandez (real name has been changed), many topics regarding second language acquisition were discussed in response to a protocol of twenty-six questions provided by the lead author for a mandatory case study assignment. Topics such as difficulty in adjusting to U.S. schools and society, lack of knowledge of the English language, motivation for learning English, and the demands of comprehending two different cultural contexts were discussed. Cultural values and experiences pertaining to the heritage culture of the interviewee were also shared.

At the time the case study research was conducted, the interviewee gave an extensive description of his upbringing in Mexico and in the United States, his experiences in the American school system as a participant in an English as a second language (ESL) program, and the culture shock he experienced uprooting from one environment to the other. Additional issues were discussed in greater detail including the informant's difficulties and challenges in acquiring English as a second language, understanding different cultural values, and daily experiences in U.S. American society.

The interviewee's English was fully comprehensible at the time of the interview. It would be difficult for a stranger to assume that Spanish was Diego's first language. Furthermore, the informant successfully completed high school and attained an associate's degree at a community college in the state of Texas.

Diego grew up initially in Monclava, Mexico, and moved to Texas when he was thirteen years old. At home, the interviewee's family strictly spoke Spanish. Growing up, Diego recalled having literacy materials in his home in his heritage language. However, the interviewee confessed that throughout his upbringing he had no interest in reading for either personal interests or educational purposes. As far as reading materials in English, the interviewee did not have additional print resources in the second language apart from those provided by his public school in Texas.

In his early teenage life, the informant's mother had filed for a divorce from her husband, and once the divorce was finalized, the informant's mother moved to the United States to seek employment. She arranged to have Diego move to Texas with her when he was thirteen years of age, after his biological father had passed away. At this point, the interviewee had successfully completed the 7th grade in his home country.

Going to school in Monclava, Mexico, Diego was interested in learning English as a second language. He commented with disappointment that the classroom setting in Mexico did not prepare him enough for actually living in the United States. As a result of this, Diego experienced extreme difficulties while moving to Texas and adjusting to the new society. Still, the informant was determined to acquire the English language with full proficiency because he wanted to prosper in his new homeland.

The interviewee's mother and stepfather did not feel the same way. They had more difficulty learning English, and the interviewee described how they only learned English in the work context, which didn't provide enough exposure to the language in order to become proficient. While Diego's mother was unable to linguistically support her son, he remarked that she never failed to lovingly support, care, and provide for him in the United States.

The interviewee attended school for five years in the public school system in Texas before moving on to gain additional education at a local community college. During his time in public school, Diego was identified as an ESL student, reaping the benefits of being in an ESL program. Reflecting back on his experiences in an ESL classroom, the informant shared how he enjoyed seeing his ESL teacher care for all of the students and their cultures displayed in the classroom environment. The educator's positive attitude, interactive teaching, and commitment to help her students gave the informant great confidence to learn. Still, the interviewee found learning the English language to be particularly difficult.

When the informant was asked what the simplest part of learning English was, he responded that there was no single aspect of studying English that he found "easy." Diego stated that his struggle in learning academic English pertained to the comprehension of more rigorous vocabulary and specific skills inherent to certain content areas. He noted that it was difficult for him to hear, interpret, write, read, and converse simultaneously. It was his belief that it was his teacher's positive influence that assisted him in continuing his academic pursuit of learning English as a second language.

In his ESL classroom, Diego found himself most engaged in the learning material when it was culturally relevant. Additionally, he enjoyed learning when elements of his culture or language were included in the curriculum or individual lessons. The informant noted how he especially enjoyed learning about holidays celebrated in America with which he was not familiar.

The interviewee spoke about how he appreciated that the administrators and teachers he had in the Texas public school system celebrated his culture through holidays, such as Cinco de Mayo and through recognizing the Hispanic Heritage Month. Moreover, the informant's teachers sometimes provided helpful materials in the form of homework for both the informant and his mother. The majority of these resources included creative assignments that were offered in both English and Spanish. While not everything was translated for him and his family, he did find the translations that were provided to be helpful in studying English.

Cultural values are very important to Diego and his family. He noted that even after moving to the United States he kept strong ties to his home country and his family still living there. To this day, the informant holds fast to his culture. Part of his encouragement to remain tied to his home country was because a large majority of the informant's family still resides in Mexico.

Diego indicated that he experienced some culture shock upon moving to the United States, stating that he realized how different the American and Hispanic cultures were. He described the Hispanic culture to be much more celebratory than the culture he has witnessed in America. Regardless of the shock he experienced the acculturation process, Diego stated that he and his family still kept traditions and customs they had in Mexico. This action reduced the stress associated with the culture shock he encountered upon first arriving in the United States.

While the informant experienced many difficulties in coping with moving from his home country, adjusting to a new society, and learning the English language, he mentioned that he was thankful that he began learning English while in Mexico. Learning the language early in his development assisted him in comprehending, reading, writing, and speaking the English language. The interviewee concluded that he firmly believed his English to be fluent. Overall, the interviewee's aspiration for all ESL teachers is that they would provide hope for their students, supported by patience and understanding for the students who are struggling to learn English.

Currently, Diego is married and has established his life in the state of Texas. Still keeping his native culture and language alive through communicating with family, friends, and others in society, the informant has become a proficient bilingual. Diego Hernandez strongly believes that the fight to keep culture alive and the encouragement he received from his mother and educators assisted him in successfully acquiring English as a second language.

THE LITERATURE REVIEW

Among the most crucial influences in the education of ELLs are the relationships and interactions with significant persons, such as teachers, parents, and caretakers. Urie Bronfenbrenner, a psychologist recognized for his development of the ecological systems theory, defined a microsystem as a person's immediate interactions that affect development (Berk, 2010, p. 20). In the context of acquiring a second language, an ELL's microsystem, including the individual's parents and educators, has the ability to positively influence or inhibit an individual from making gains in second language development.

Culturally responsive teaching (CRT), as defined by Irvine (2009), is recognized as "effective teaching in a culturally diverse classroom." Gay (2002) further noted that CRT represents a teaching philosophy that recognizes and accepts students' cultural heritage and seeks to build connections of relevance between the school and home with the goal of making school success accessible to every student. The affirmation and encouragement of heritage cultures and languages is critical in the teaching of linguistically and culturally diverse students (Sleeter, 2012).

While culturally responsive pedagogy alone cannot ensure a student's academic success, it has been found to contribute in meaningful ways to overall achievement in second language acquisition (Ladson-Billings, 2001; Kea, Campbell-Whatley, & Richards, 2004; Richards, Brown, & Forde, 2004; Gay, 2002). The idea of culturally relevant and responsive teaching is also intended to provide students with the ability to develop a "broader sociopolitical consciousness" outside of the classroom setting in regards to cultural norms, values, education, and language acquisition (Ladson-Billings,

2001, p. 162). The participant's responses in his interview supported this notion as he stated that while his formal education of the English language was helpful, it was in the social arena outside of school, at work or with his English speaking peers, where he primarily learned English as a second language.

Researchers have stated that teaching in a culturally relevant and responsive manner encourages students to engage in the classroom context, where they will be able to envision themselves and their experiences reflected in the curriculum, thus having enhanced motivation (Shahid, 2009). In spite of the great diversity that exists within the student population in the United States, it is essential to note that ELLs rarely see themselves or their experiences reflected in the school curriculum. Ovando, Combs, and Collier (2006) noted that the small amount of information or materials representative of different cultures that is included in the curriculum is often erroneous. Gandara and Contreras (2009) maintained that an uninformed teacher may negatively impact a students' academic future by failing to address the unique educational challenges encountered by Latino adolescents. Including accurate information about diverse languages, cultures, and histories underscores a valuing of individual and group heritages, creating a sense of acceptance and welcome that is vital to the success of ELLs.

Cowart (2007) suggested that there are two possible routes to the foremost objective of scholastic attainment for all students. One path is full of irritation, anxiety, and failure for both students and teachers when there is too little consideration given to the additive process of acculturation as the best choice for adapting to a new language and culture. The other path is still filled with challenges, but without the cultural borders that are sometimes built up by teachers who inhibit cultural expression by insisting on a linguistically and culturally subtractive process of assimilation (Gollnick & Chinn, 2006).

The participant found that teaching styles and instructional materials that were inclusive of aspects of the Hispanic culture or language contributed to his educational gains. Having the opportunity to make connections with what was culturally significant, while acquiring new concepts found in the English language, led to further feats in second language acquisition for the interviewee.

Furthermore, teaching with culture in mind does not exclusively address academic achievement, but is also relevant to the preservation of culture and raising cultural awareness (Shahid, 2009). Such an approach to the classroom and teaching encourages students to pursue an adjustment process of acculturation, which is additive in nature, instead of the subtractive assimilation route. Implementing culturally responsive pedagogy for language minority students who are learning English as a second language protects them from the stress of an assimilative environment.

Providing access to culturally relevant books and resources effectively supports skill development and academic progress for ELLs (Rodríguez, 2009). Books of this sort provide familiar ground for ELLs to comprehend texts and acquire language successfully. Children tend to be more successful when reading about topics and issues they have experienced (Freeman & Freeman, 2004). One point the interviewee emphasized pertaining to his education in the United States was the fact that some of his teachers provided materials that related to his linguistic and cultural heritage.

Parental involvement can increase the educational performance of ELLs. However, facilitating parental involvement among parents of nonnative English speaking families is frequently challenging to attain (Panferov, 2010). This could be the result of many factors including communication gaps between the parents and faculty, cultural variations, or even the parent's focus on other matters, such as their occupations and providing for their families (Good, Masewicz, & Vogel, 2010).

The parents of recently arrived immigrants and refugees may have vastly different expectations of the teachers, their children, the school, and themselves as parents. Beliefs about the various roles of those involved in the education of children typically vary by culture (Cowart, 2007). Regardless of the difficulties of engaging parents in the lives of their children's education, it is important to note that participation from the caretaker is significant for the English language learner (Panferov, 2010).

Not only does parental involvement motivate ELLs in their language acquisition, but also interest on behalf of the parents may lead to the maintenance of the heritage language (Kung, 2013). Participation from both fathers and mothers includes many forms. Parents can actively engage in activities with their children that pertain to their education, such as reading alongside children, either in the home language or English. They may try to learn English with their children.

Parents might elect to enroll their families in bilingual family literacy programs where community members, as well as teachers, can support families in learning a second language (Peercy, Martin-Beltran, & Daniel, 2013). Students who see their caretakers making a dedicated effort to learn English, or simply support them during second language acquisition, have increased motivation to advance in their knowledge of English (Portes & Rumbaut, 2006).

Nieto and Bode (2011) remark that a deterrent to academic achievement for culturally and linguistically diverse students is the restricted role of parents which is sometimes limited by school structure and procedures and sometimes narrow because of the different interpretations held by diverse parents regarding the parent–teacher relationship. Diego commented that materials were often not translated into the language of the home. This practice is not only destined to inhibit parental involvement, it is also contradictory to the *Lau v. Nichols* (1974) court decision in which the judge ordered schools to overcome educational barriers caused by a lack of proficiency in the English language. The practice is also in conflict with Title VI of the *Civil Rights Act of 1964* which forbids denial of equal access to education because of a student's limited proficiency in English. Title VI prohibits discrimination on the basis of national origin, which includes language-based discrimination by any entity that receives federal funds (Smith, 2014).

When schools use the same tactics for reaching out to all parents without considering cultural and language differences, they frequently fail in the important work of facilitating parent participation. When working with students and teachers in diverse settings, several promising practices were observed by one of the authors. The administrators and teachers at a school in a large school district located in the southwestern part of the United States and possessing a sizable population of ELLs were disappointed at the lack of parental involvement among the parents of the linguistically diverse students. The educators decided to go out into the community and hold parent teacher meetings where the parents were comfortable—at community centers and clinics. The number of parents who began to participate in meetings grew rapidly.

While teaching English as a second language in middle school for substantial numbers of recently arrived refugee students from Southeast Asia and immigrants from Mexico and Central American countries, teachers at the school were encouraged by the principal to make home visits with interpreter aides during their planning periods so that contact might be made with parents who were uncomfortable coming to the school for meetings. This practice led to invitations from parents to attend cultural celebrations and events.

Once the teachers began going to some of the festivities, the parents appeared to find the school setting less intimidating and began to feel more at ease discussing concerns about their children. Thus, parental involvement among parents who are culturally and linguistically diverse is possible if educators and administrators are willing to differentiate their approaches to working with parents in the same way that they are expected to differentiate instruction for children.

Where the research showed that parental involvement leads to great gains in language acquisition, the interviewee somewhat contradicted the findings. Although the interviewee indicated that he continues to maintain strong ties with his culture, heritage, and primary language, he clearly stated that his mother's desire to learn English as a second language was not as strong as his was.

The interviewee described how it was difficult for his mother to learn English since she only "learned English in the work context," and therefore, she did not possess the same motivation to acquire English as a second language. For the interviewee, the fuel that drove his desire to acquire English as a second language came from the aspiration to thrive in a new country where he most wanted to live, and to do well in life. The interviewee also had a small amount of prior knowledge of English before entering an American public school and being placed in an ESL classroom.

Microsystem influences, such as educators or parents, have the ability to positively influence a student's acquisition of a second language. By creating a culturally and linguistically accepting environment in the classroom and teaching in a manner that incorporates students' heritages into the curriculum, ELLs will be better positioned for academic success in the content areas and in second language acquisition. Likewise, having support and encouragement from parents and caretakers provides additional positive support in language acquisition.

Both practices will serve to motivate and provide the type of academic, cultural, and language support that will facilitate enhanced educational performance for English language learners. When combined with positive social learning tools, additional motivation, and practice, ELLs will make significant progress in acquiring a second language and becoming all that they might be.

THE GUIDING QUESTIONS

Based upon the information provided by the interviewee and the existing research, the questions below may be useful for administrators and other educators interested in implementing a program of Culturally Relevant and Responsive Teaching in their classrooms and schools. Several of the questions are intended to assist with reflection and planning for greater parental involvement of parents of ELLs.

1. What procedures are in place in your school district to inform district personnel regarding the arrival and movement of newcomers? Why would it be beneficial for all personnel to possess this knowledge?
2. How might teachers be encouraged to embark on the type of multicultural journey that is described by Nieto and Bode (2011) as being both outward (learning about other groups and individuals) and inward (identifying and challenging previously learned and held stereotypical notions about diverse groups and individuals)? How would this change classroom climate in a way that is beneficial to learning?
3. What professional development is available to assist teachers and administrators in developing cross-cultural sensitivity? If none exists, develop a plan for creating and institutionalizing this type of staff development. What should be included in this sort of cultural awareness and sensitivity training?

4. What programs are in place for assisting educators in developing skills for differentiating instruction and teaching in a culturally responsive manner even during an era of high-stakes testing when energies and resources are diverted away from those who need additional linguistic and academic support?
5. What procedures are in place in your school district for engaging and including non-English speaking parents? What are three innovative strategies for facilitating parental involvement among culturally and linguistically diverse parents? What are two benefits for doing so?
6. What are the special language programs available in your school district and how are they designed? What are the most essential components comprising each program. How might CRT be included in these programs?

FINAL CONSIDERATIONS

As educators and administrators ponder how to incorporate a program of culturally relevant and responsive teaching and contemplate the best approach for enhancing greater parental involvement, possible responses to the questions listed above may serve to guide the development of effective plans.

1. The first step for educators in planning for culturally relevant instruction should include ascertaining whether the school district has an established protocol to follow to inform teachers about newcomers they will have in class. Since relationships and interactions are among the most crucial influences in the successful acculturation and second language acquisition of ELLs, it would be essential for educators to be cognizant of the students' backgrounds, and needs. Schools and teachers will want to know whether a student has been able to attend school in the home country and reach a degree of native language literacy that would support the development of literacy skills in the second language. Knowledge of an ELL's prior cultural experiences would help teachers to more appropriately interpret the student's academic, social, and linguistic behaviors. Each administrator and teacher ought to elect to learn about cultures and languages in order to bring accurate and significant cultural information to the classroom setting.
2. The administrators within a school must commit to a program of multicultural teaching and reflective action. Subsequently, the expectation for teachers within that school should be that each educator would embark on a multicultural journey that is simultaneously inward and outward. Educators should become aware of the various

cultures in each classroom and find ways to incorporate world heritages into the curriculum.

Critical reflection about the importance of integrating students' cultures into the classroom curriculum would be necessary. Without the dedication of the administration within a school, it is unlikely that there would be much endorsement for a program of culturally relevant and responsive teaching. Allowing students to see their cultural experiences reflected in the curriculum would usher in a heightened sense of acceptance and belonging for the ELLs. Motivation for learning would be increased because of the students' greater self-esteem.

3. If no plan for developing cross-cultural sensitivity is in place, administrators and educators working together may begin to identify the type of knowledge they require in order to teach in a culturally responsive manner and to include students' cultures and languages in the classroom. At the same time, steps may be taken to find consultants who could assist the educators in developing their new multicultural plan.

4. If professional development regarding how to suitably differentiate instruction is unavailable, a team of teachers and administrators at the school should cultivate a plan for fashioning staff development that will enable teachers to differentiate instruction while teaching in a culturally relevant and responsive way.

5. Educators must look for meaningful ways in which to make culturally and linguistically diverse parents feel a greater sense of welcome at their children's schools. Suggested practices include keeping parents updated about what is going on in the classroom in languages they comprehend, informing parents about what the students are learning, and if possible, providing additional resources or recommendations for the parents pertaining to what the student is learning. Parents can be invited to participate in ways and places that are actually inviting to them. They should be encouraged to read with their children in the heritage language and/or English. This is not an either/or situation. Reading in both languages will be mutually beneficial. The benefits to such actions will be a sense of empowerment for parents and having a voice regarding the education of their children along with a strengthened partnership in striving for excellence and equity.

6. After learning about the special language programs available to linguistically and culturally diverse students within a school district, it will be essential for educators to consider which elements of culturally relevant teaching they want to implement. Because a program of this type will require time for development of an effective plan, as well as ongoing professional preparation of teachers, a sound working design would have a yearly phase-in component with guidelines concerning which components to incorporate for each year in the plan.

Initially and throughout program development, it would be important to identify sources of culturally relevant books and resources in each classroom and to find resources for purchasing the books. Similarly, teachers would want to become familiar with the stories and content in order to effectively include the information in what is being taught.

PROTOCOL OF INTERVIEW QUESTIONS

Demographic information for interviewee:

Gender: _____ Ethnicity: _____
Age: _____ Native language: _____
Number of years in attendance at U.S. public schools: ____

1. What language did you speak at home as a child?
2. At what age did you come to live in the United States?
3. Did you have reading materials in your heritage language in your home while growing up?
4. Did you have reading materials in English at home while attending U.S. public schools?
5. Describe your initial attitude regarding learning English as a second language? Did your parents share a similar attitude toward English?
6. Did you live in another country prior to arriving in the United States? If so, which country?_____ Why did your family move to the United States?
7. After completing which grade in your home country did you arrive in the United States?
8. Did you maintain strong ties with your home country? Please explain.
9. Did you learn English as a second language in a formal setting, an informal setting, or a combination of both?
10. What did you like best about your language arts/reading/English/ESL class?
11. What was the easiest part of learning to read and write in English?
12. What was the most difficult aspect of learning to speak, read, and write in English?
13. How do you view your current ability, identity, and usage of your second language?
14. How would you summarize your experiences learning a second language?
15. What do you perceive to be the major differences between your first language and English, your second language? (Phonology, morphology, word order)

16. How did societal pressures, local politics, and school policies affect your language learning?
17. What did you like to learn about in your language arts or ESL classroom?
18. What did you enjoy doing outside of school?
19. How would you compare your cultural heritage with that of the United States?
20. Describe your relationship with your school-age peers who were not members of your ethnic or language group. How did other students in class perceive English language learners in general?
21. How do you think you learn best?
22. Was there anything you wish had been different in your English language arts or ESL classroom?
23. What did your teacher(s) do that really helped you to understand how to read and write in English? What types of support or materials were provided to you? How did your teachers communicate with your parents? How did your teachers help you to celebrate and maintain your culture?
24. What could your teacher have done to help you improve in the area of English language acquisition?
25. Did you ever read about or listen to stories written by or about people from your country in the language arts classroom? (Ask for examples if the answer is yes) How did that make you feel?
26. What do you want all teachers to know about you, your culture, and your language?

GUIDELINES FOR CULTURE AND LANGUAGE INTERVIEW

1. Select your interviewee carefully.

   - Must be culturally and linguistically different from you
   - Can spend enough time with you to respond to questions and discuss thoroughly
   - Is proficient enough in English to respond thoughtfully to questions

2. Find a quiet, private place for the interview. Neutral territory is usually best for the interview.
3. Interview your subject in private with no other people present or listening.
4. The interview must be conducted face-to-face. Email interviews are not appropriate and will not be accepted.

5. Review the questions in advance and be prepared to rephrase questions.
6. Let the interviewee talk. This is his/her story. Refrain from completing answers or answering questions for him or her. Any show of opinion or judgment will alter the interviewee's answers.
7. If a question does not pertain to your interviewee, move on to the next question.
8. Build a trust relationship with your interviewee. This will enhance the quality of the responses.
9. Remain calm even if your interviewee says something you perceive to be incorrect or offensive. Remember, we want his/her story, whatever it may be. Now is not the time to correct or debate someone's perspective or beliefs.
10. Pay close attention. Show that you are interested and listening.
11. Listen for responses that naturally lead to further questioning.
12. Seek clarification for any answers that are unclear to you.
13. Remain in control of the interview.
14. Thank your interviewee for providing invaluable insights.

REFERENCES

Berk, L. E. (2010). *Exploring lifespan development* (2nd ed.). J. Mosher (Ed.). Boston, MA: Pearson Education.

Cowart, M. T. (2007). Loss and hope: Challenges in acculturation for refugee children in the United States. In P. Dam & M. T. Cowart (Eds.), *Intercultural understanding* (pp. 1-20). Arlington, VA: Canh Nam.

Cowart, M. T. (2012). Supporting refugee English language learners during acculturation and second language acquisition. In M. T. Cowart & G. Anderson (Eds.), *English Language Learners in 21st Century Classrooms: Challenges and Expectations* (pp. 11-33). Arlington, VA: Canh Nam.

Freeman, Y., & Freeman, D. (2004). Connecting students to culturally relevant texts. *Talking Points, 15(2)*, 7-11. Retrieved from: http://www.ncte.org/library/NCTEFiles/Resources/Journals/TP/0152-aprilmay04/TP0152Connecting.pdf

Gandara, P., & Contreras, F. (2009). *The Latino education crisis: The consequences of failed social policies*. Cambridge, MA: Harvard University Press.

Gay, G. (2002). Preparing for culturally responsive teaching. *Journal of Teacher Education, 53(2)*, 106-116.

Gollnick, D. M., & Chinn, P. C. (2006). *Multicultural education in a pluralistic society*. Upper Saddle River, NJ: Pearson, Merrill, Prentice Hall.

Good, M. E., Masewicz, S., & Vogel, L. (2010). Latino English language learners: Bridging achievement and cultural gaps between schools and families. *Journal of Latinos & Education, 9(4)*, 321-339. Retrieved from: http://ezproxy.twu.edu:2339/ehost/pdfviewer/pdfviewer?sid=e7a1673d-0c74-4dae-af7c-3cb341e9eb7a%40sessionmgr4002&vid=6&hid=4212

Immigration Policy Center of the American Immigration Council. (n.d.) *How the United States immigration system works: A fact sheet*. Retrieved from: www.immigrationpolicycenter.org

Irvine, J. J. (2009). Relevant: Beyond the basics. *Teaching tolerance, 36*. Retrieved from: http://www.tolerance.org/magazine/number-36-fall-2009/feature/relevant-beyond-basics

Kea, C., Campbell-Whatley, G. D., & Richards, H. V. (2005). *Becoming culturally-*

responsive educators: Rethinking teacher education pedagogy. National Center for Culturally Responsive Systems, U.S. Department of Education, Office of Special Education Programs: Award No. H326EO20003.

Kung, F. (2013). Bilingualism and the second generation: Investigating the effects and methods of heritage language maintenance and second language acquisition. *English Teaching & Learning, 37*(3), 107-145. Retrieved from: http://ezproxy.twu.edu:2225/ehost/pdfviewer/pdfviewer?sid=00ac219a-b4d2-4776-81ea-a855aa66ffdb%40sessionmgr110&vid=10&hid=127

Ladson-Billings, G. (2001). But that's just good teaching! The case for culturally relevant pedagogy. *Theory into practice, 34*(3), 159-165. Retrieved from: http://ezproxy.twu.edu:2048/login?url=http://ezproxy.twu.edu:2060/login.aspx?direct=true&db=tfh&AN=5655844&site=ehost-live&scope=site

Martin, D. C., & Yankay, J. E. (2014). *Refugees and asylees: 2013.* (Annual Flow Report.) U.S. Department of Homeland Security Office of Immigration Statistics. Retrieved from: www.dhs.gov/immigrationstatistics

Meyer, P. J., Seelke, C. R., Taft-Morales, M., & Margesson, R. (2015). *Unaccompanied children from Central America: Foreign policy considerations.* Washington, DC: Congressional Research Service.

Nieto, S., & Bode, P. (2011). *Affirming diversity: The sociopolitical context of multicultural education.* Boston, MA: Allyn & Bacon.

Ovando, C., Combs, M. C., & Collier, V. (2006) *Bilingual and ESL classrooms: Teaching in multicultural contexts* (4th edition). Boston: McGraw Hill.

Panferov, S. (2010). Increasing ELL parental involvement in our schools: Learning from the parents. *Theory into practice, 49*(2),106-112. Retrieved from: http://ezproxy.twu.edu:2339/ehost/pdfviewer/pdfviewer?sid=e7a1673d-0c74-4dae-af7c-3cb341e9eb7a%40sessionmgr4002&vid=4&hid=4212

Peercy, M. M., Martin-Beltran, M., & Daniel, S. M. (2013). Learning together: Creating a community of practice to support English language learner literacy. *Language, culture and curriculum, 26*(3), 284-299.

Portes, A., & Rumbaut, R. (2006). Immigrant America: A portrait (3rd Edition). Berkley, CA: University of California Press.

Richards, H. V., Brown, A. F., & Forde, T. B. (2004). *Addressing diversity in schools: Culturally responsive pedagogy.* Denver: National Center for Culturally Responsive Educational Systems.

Rodríguez, A. D. (2009). Culturally relevant books: Connecting Hispanic students to the curriculum. *GiST: Education and learning research journal, 3,* 11-29. Retrieved from: https://twu.illiad.oclc.org/illiad/illiad.dll?Action=10&Form=75&Value=124873

Shahid, H. (2009). The effects of implementing culturally relevant teaching, two-column note-taking, and graphic organizers in the pedagogical stances and instructions of secondary content teachers. *Dissertation Abstracts International, A: The Humanities and Social Sciences,* 4618. Retrieved from: http://zproxy.twu.edu:2048/docview/85698719?accountid=7102 (85698719; 200921249).

Sleeter, C. (2012). Confronting the marginalization of culturally responsive pedagogy. *Urban Education, 47,* 562-584.

Smith, N. (2014). *English as a second language: Age appropriate placements.* Cumberland County Schools, Fayetteville, NC. Retrieved from: esl.ccs.k12.nc.us/age-appropriate-placements

Weiss-Armush, A. M. (2010). DFW International Community Alliance 2010 progress report. Retrieved from: http://www.dfwinternational.org

Zong, J., & Batilova, J. (2015). Frequently requested statistics on immigrants and immigration in the United States. Migration Policy Institute. Retrieved from: http://www.migrationpolicy.org

II

Issues That Affect the School Campus

Chapter Four

The American-Type International School

A Question of Ethics

Warren G. Ortloff, Luz Marina Escobar, and Ava Muñoz

United States regionally accredited international schools can be found throughout the world and have a few major characteristics in common, they all offer an American type of education; use curriculum and instructional materials developed in America; and must meet and maintain state-side regional accreditation association standards. Like in America, diversity among students and school staff are the norm, but often to a greater degree as families and faculty come from many nations while bringing with them their own expectations regarding what a good education should look like.

This case study follows a PreK-12 school head (principal) while addressing faculty, parental, and School Board issues that are so intertwined that there seems to be no easy solution. Situations offer ethical dilemmas involving teachers' professional behavior, due process and termination issues, quality of supervision, and issues of simple fairness.

THE CASE STUDY

The World Traveling Administrator

George Smith loved traveling and experiencing different cultures. His desire to always be on the move was probably brought on by spending much of his childhood as a dependent of a career naval officer whose family accompanied him on his travels throughout Europe and North Africa. Another interest to George was all things related to education, so he entered the teaching profession and eventually taught at all school levels from elementary through high school in the subjects of physical education, special education, and the sciences. Eventually, George's interest turned to school administration where he served several years as a high school assistant principal and athletic/activity director at a Midwestern rural public school. Again, George desired an even greater challenge, ideally one that would combine his desire for travel with his love of education.

By chance George met a teacher in his district who had served a number of years overseas at private schools whose purpose was primarily to educate the children of Americans working overseas. This challenge interested him and he discussed the possibility with his wife. As a result, George and his wife attended an international teacher recruiting fair where he interviewed for international teaching positions and as an afterthought, a school director position at a very small American international school serving expatriate employee dependents of namely multinational companies and Christian missionaries in Africa. To his surprise, George was invited to visit the school with his wife for an interview with the Board of Directors and to meet the school community.

Excited about the possibility of leading a private international school overseas that was incorporated in the United States, George immediately went online to check out the school and found that it was located in West Africa. George investigated further and learned that the school was located in the country's capitol city and was founded in 1955 by missionaries. Over time, control and influence within the school had been increasingly provided by multinational corporations and foreign embassies.

The country's Ministry of Education did not interfere with school operations other than recognizing its existence because there were no host country nationals attending the school. American students were the majority at 35% with 24 other nationalities represented. The school was well funded with student tuition averaging 15,000 USD per academic year and because of the presence of embassy employee children, security received the highest priority. The school had 200 students, PreK-12, with 37 full-time faculty and only one administrator who reported directly to the school's Board of Directors. Teaching staff was comprised of 26 Americans, 9 Canadians, and 2 from other countries. All faculty were certified teachers in their home country and the school was beginning the process of seeking accreditation through a regional accreditation agency in the United States.

English was the language of instruction with an average elementary class size of 15 students and 16 students in the secondary school. There was a half-time school counselor and a full-time school nurse and librarian. The campus was situated on 100 hectares with 6 buildings, 30 classrooms, 2 computer labs, 100 computers, and 7,500 library volumes. A variety of extracurricular programs were offered, e.g., excursions, yearbook, and a sports program that featured soccer, swimming, volleyball, badminton and basketball. Examinations included the SAT, TOEFL, PSAT and the Advanced Placement program was offered to secondary students.

George was sold on the possibility of becoming the school's director and shared his enthusiasm with his wife. He soon relayed to the Board of Directors their desire to accept the Board's invitation to visit. After a flight that seemed to last forever, George and his wife arrived at their destination and after a short night's sleep they arrived on campus. They toured the campus and for two days met with both parents and students and then followed up with informal and formal meetings with the Board of Directors.

All interactions with the school community were quite positive and George and his wife left the two-day affair feeling they would be a good match with the school-community's aspirations of: greater school growth in both student numbers and physical facilities; increased student academic achievement; alignment of the entire curriculum; and increased community involvement by the school.

George remembered his wife asking during the return flight home whether he felt ready to assume this level of responsibility having had no administrative support, not even a principal or central office administrative staff. George replied "Yes, I am" while realizing that he would have to "learn on the fly" while answering to a Board of Directors (School Board). The Board president called two days after George returned home and offered him the position as school director to which he immediately accepted. George was never one to hesitate when presented with a challenge.

The American School Director

George's first two years at the school presented a real challenge as this was his first school position where the "buck stopped with him" and he reported directly to a Board of Directors. The politics were real and his decisions had real time consequences: however, through it all, he tried and did make thoughtful decisions based upon what was in the best interest of student learning.

The first two years of George's tenure were productive. He made a great deal of progress toward achieving school goals and school/community support was present. During this time the working relationship between the Board and George were excellent mainly because of a close personal relationship with the Board president; however, George received no written Board annual evaluations, only informal feedback during Board meetings.

George believed that the school teaching staff and administration were a true team in every measure. The relationship between and among students, parents, teachers, administration, Board of Directors, and outside community were very positive as most seemed to buy in and support school endeavors and goals. Teachers seemed to appreciate George's leadership style and respected his easy going, straight-forward and can-do demeanor.

George began his third year of employment as director and sole administrator of the now 300 student PreK-12 American International School. There was an air of excitement and optimism running throughout the entire school community and George just knew that this school year would be one of accomplishment. Accomplishment, in part, through significant progress being made toward achieving state-side regional accreditation and of bringing the school community together through a planned expansion of the school's role as the center of education and social activity for the expatriate community.

The New Hires

George was excited about welcoming a new experienced teaching couple to the school's staff under a two-year contract. This couple showed great promise and had a record of educational and community leadership, a trait that he considered important to small school success. He was especially excited that one person was a physical education teacher and coach who would also assume the new, but extremely important position of athletic/activities coordinator.

George was proud to have successfully sold this new athletic/activities coordinator position to the Board of Directors through making the case that the school was serving as the center of social and educational activities for the entire expatriate community. He reasoned that with a growing number of expatriates moving into the area, the school should be expected to take on a greater role toward meeting community educational and activity/social needs. This expectation was supported by the school-community and Board, which generated a great deal of discussion as to the need for a community center on campus.

George understood that the school community in the past had accepted the expanded role of the school because expatriates wanted and expected the school to serve as their "home away from home." International companies desired an American international school that would provide a "world class" education in order to attract and retain outstanding employees and encourage them to bring their families. They recognized that an intact family led to greater job satisfaction and job stability.

The Athletics/Coordinator and Coach

George was aware that as an American international school overseas, its presence made life bearable for many families, with or without children. He thought having an effective athletic/activities coordinator and coach who was motivated to meet the community's needs and expectations were important for the entire school-community. It seemed to George that as soon as Sam arrived on campus, he had what appeared to be a real winner in the position.

Sam was a man of slight stature from the United States. He was a strong-willed and independent individual whose spouse was on the high school teaching staff. Sam and his wife (Mary) were a very popular teaching couple since their arrival on campus and in short duration commanded considerable respect and influence within the school community. Sam quickly dug into his role as athletic/activities coordinator; making contacts, developing programs, and promoting school-community activities. George appreciated the "can-do" attitude and considered Sam generally quite effective, but sensed even from the beginning of the school year he was losing control and influence over the school's athletic and activities initiatives and programs.

Difficult Situations Ensue

By the beginning of September, George realized that he had a serious problem on his hands to which he did not have any quick fix. Sam refused to keep George adequately informed as to the plans for the school's present and future athletic and activity programs. The plans that Sam did share were often inaccurate and placed George in difficult situations, often financially, where George would appear to be actively trying to block all the "great things" Sam and the school community were trying to accomplish. When Sam was not permitted to carry through with an activity, Sam would take the opportunity to verbally place blame directly on George through making his disagreements public.

It seemed the athletic/activities coordinator and coach had a real problem with authority. George continually tried reasoning with Sam through asking probing questions to draw out constructive dialogue regarding athletic/activities plans and activities with no success throughout September and October. Sam intentionally shared less and less information during the weekly planning meetings and discussions became increasingly heated. At one such planning meeting, Sam stated to George that he "came to teach internationally in order to retire and did not expect to work hard and be bothered by anyone."

George began documenting Sam's unacceptable conduct beginning in the middle of September and followed up with "formal" letters that addressed specific areas of concern along with specific expectations and agreements made. Insubordination became a major concern. George had kept the Board president informed of these concerns regarding Sam's conduct since the end of September realizing that should Sam's unacceptable behavior not cease, serious administrative and Board action might be warranted.

School Security Incident

At the very beginning of November, a serious school security issue had been reported to George by a parent that threatened the personal safety of students participating in school and after school athletic activities. Since the school was in a rural setting adjacent to a large wooded public park, security was always a real concern. Sam was using the wooded, park area for physical education and athletic conditioning, which included cross-country running, during and after school. George on one occasion witnessed Sam working in his office while the cross-country team was running in the park off campus without supervision.

George took pride in knowing what was always happening at the school as he regularly inspected the school building, surrounding grounds, and made regular teacher classroom observations. On more than one occasion he observed that the back gate of the school leading to the public park was unlocked and sometimes even wide open. Custodial staff reported that Sam was opening the back gate on a daily basis while failing to close and lock it. Since this security concern was reported, George had included this concern during the weekly planning sessions and actually made it clear to Sam through a written memo that the back gate to the park was to be closed and locked at all times and that cross-country activities would only take place under his direct supervision.

George throughout November, both formally and informally, respectfully reminded Sam of this school-safety expectation, but there was no change in behavior as the outside gate continued to be left unlocked and the lack of student supervision remained an issue. Since September, George had been forced to follow through with informal and formal office conferences along with corresponding written reprimands with copies placed in Sam's personnel file.

Informing the School Board

George regularly kept the Board president aware of his concerns and actions regarding Sam's behavior from the beginning, but they did not become an official executive Board agenda item until November. After presenting his case to the Board in the third week of November, George sensed concern among some of the members as to why he had not taken immediate affirmative action as soon as the problem was not corrected. Most of the Board members were top managers of multinational companies who in their line of work would not tolerate for a minute, employees who refused to follow directives and meet expectations. Taking swift, decisive personnel action was the norm.

George had to, in a respectful way, remind the Board members that schools are social and community-wide organizations, and as such, any turmoil has the potential to disrupt teaching which could have a negative effect on their employees' children and their learning. The Board was advised that if any serious personal action was taken, namely termination, it needed to be "smartly and timely" done.

Strike 3: Terminating the Coach

On December 1, the Board requested a "special executive session" and asked George if the situation with Sam had improved. George stated "No" and in fact it had gotten worse, resulting in stress among some school staff while some parents were talking among themselves. It was evident to George that the Board had been discussing the problem among themselves when they stated to George that they wanted "decisive action with regards to Sam." The Board made it clear that this action included immediate termination. The Board directed George to compose a letter of termination, which would be signed by a majority of the Board and by himself.

George was directed to present to Sam the termination letter at the conclusion of the final school day before Christmas break. George dreaded that day and expected the worst with the execution of the termination letter. When that day came, George summoned Sam to his office and presented the letter. After a heated discussion, Sam left the office quite upset and discussed his termination with anybody who would listen: faculty; staff; parents; and even students.

The termination caused quite a scene as it appeared to be unexpected, especially by parents, students, teachers, and yes, the terminated teacher. However, George suspected that with a Board composed of members all having children attending the school, there was considerable opportunity for word to get out in advance to parents and even students, and it probably did.

George's Dilemma

George found himself in the middle of an administrative nightmare, one that he preferred not to have taken place as it did. He felt forced by the Board into taking administrative action at an inopportune time. He further felt that it would be unethical for him to share with the community the reasons for the termination. George knew what was coming, but there were even more surprises.

George's life became quite memorable following his presentation of the termination letter to Sam. Since Sam would no longer be allowed to live in teacher housing on campus, his termination for all practical purposes extended to his teaching spouse and their two children who also lived on campus and attended the school. In addition, since both teaching spouses were employed on a work visa and termination of Sam's employment presented a problem with him remaining in the country without a work visa. The Board did not want him to remain in the area where school-community disruptions could be the end result.

Following the conclusion of the last day of school before the Christmas break, news of Sam's termination traveled fast throughout the school and community. Sam and his wife did their best to fan the flames and spoke to all that would listen concerning the injustice imposed upon them and their children.

George's first visitors with concerns were the officers of the Parent–Teachers Association who demanded to know the reason for the termination. It was a short, hot, and emotional meeting, but George tried to remain calm and informed the parents that the action was, in part, an administrative matter that involved student safety concerns requiring swift administrative action. George wanted to elaborate further, but knew that he was already pushing the envelope. He finished the PTA visitation by stating that all personnel matters must remain confidential, but they were free to communicate with the teacher if they wished.

That evening following the termination, Sam stated to George that all the teachers had issues regarding how he was running the school. George made a mental note of the issues presented and challenged his statement. George asked, "Did you mean all the teachers have issues with me and my school management?" and Sam stated to the affirmative. Hearing this, George immediately called for a general faculty meeting the next morning where Sam's issues were presented to the entire faculty. The majority of teachers upon hearing the issues became upset and stated that "if these issues were a concern they would have brought it up themselves and did not need anyone to speak on their behalf."

Ominous Feeling

It was now several days into the December Christmas break and there still existed considerable rumbling within the school community. For George and his wife, this tension was only relieved somewhat by leaving for a one week ocean cruise. Half way through the cruise, George had a strange sensation that not all was well at the school. He telephoned a teacher that he trusted, a teacher with whom he often placed in charge of the school during his absence. This teacher informed him that there was a great deal of teacher, parental, and community activity on campus and some of it involved meetings with Board members.

George became aware of a rumor that Sam and his wife would return to teaching on campus following the Christmas break. Hearing this, many thoughts entered George's head, such as, would Sam return only to complete the present school year or be allowed to complete his two-year contact? What would my working relationship be with Sam and would I be able to carry on effectively with my administrative duties? What would my relationship with the Board be and would I still have authority over my teachers and support staff? What agreements were made between the Board and Sam in my absence? Would I even still have a job upon my return to the school or even have my position for a fourth year?

Community Influence Overturns Termination

Upon George's return to school the first week of January, he immediately met with the Board president to get an accurate assessment as to what took place during his absence. The Board president confirmed that Sam and his wife would return to complete the present academic year. George asked why the termination decision had been reversed and was told that parents met with Board members and convinced them to allow Sam, Mary, and their children to remain and complete the present academic year.

George found the Board's termination reversal strange since it was the Board that all along insisted that the termination take place as it did. George reminded the Board that he had advised against immediate termination as he was concerned about instilling a highly negative school climate; a climate not conducive to student learning and making progress toward achieving school accreditation. The Board president, George's greatest advocate on the Board, assured George he was still the school director and would remain in that position through the following school year. However, the Board president further stated to George that he would step down from the Board presidency at the end of the present school year.

School Board Changes

George was greatly concerned because he was going to lose his most influential Board advocate following the completion of the present school year and did not know for sure who would assume the presidency. Since Board membership is dependent upon the number of stocks (votes) a company owns in the school, votes determine Board composition and the Board president. Therefore, George suspected that a Board member from the largest stock owning company would be selected president. He further suspected that the new president would be the same Board member with whom he often had school policy disagreements, who was also the main supporter of Sam returning to the school. The prospect of George's contract extension beyond the next or 4th school year became a concern.

The Accreditation Process

The spring semester of George's third year progressed well considering the hit that he and the school climate received. George was hopeful that since the entire school community was actively engaged in the school's accreditation process coupled with his timely absence of nearly one month recruiting teachers in the United States, there would be a reduction of stress on campus.

The school community understood that much rested upon the school receiving state-side, regional accreditation and the entire community pulled together for mutual benefit. With the school population being so internationally mobile and the fact that the employed parent could be transferred to another country at a moment's notice, they understood that other international schools or even schools within their home country might not accept their children's work from a school that was not accredited.

George's Fourth and Final Year

It was the fall semester of George's fourth year as school director and he was excited about what the new academic year would bring, especially without the negative influence of Sam. The school-community seemed to calm down and there was little mention as to the difficulties experienced the year before. The new school year was off to a good start and there were no negative personal issues, but George was dismayed to learn at the beginning of the semester that the new Board president was indeed the Board member that he had issues with in the past. Board meetings proved tense for George under the new Board leadership as he sensed an adversarial relationship among the Board toward himself. Proposals presented to the Board that typically received routine approval were no longer routine.

George knew the entire school community was excited about the prospect of achieving accreditation through a regional accreditation agency in the United States this year. The accreditation visitation team, after having reviewed the school's written response to the association's standards, was scheduled to visit the school in November. The school-community felt ready for this visitation and expected a very positive result.

That November, the accreditation team arrived and spent nearly one week reviewing firsthand the school's response and actions with regards to accreditation standards. Their interview with school staff, students, parents, and Board of Directors seemed to be very positive. The visitation debriefing was also very positive as the accreditation team did not find any standards that required remediation. The school-community was excited that their school would be recommended for accreditation.

George eagerly returned from the holiday break, knowing that his school would be recommended for accreditation. However, his eagerness soon turned to reluctance and trepidation when he realized that he was not being consulted as to the Board meeting agenda as was the case during the previous three years: in fact, he had always developed the agenda in consultation with the Board president. During the January Board meeting, the issue of George's contract renewal was placed on the agenda by the Board president.

The Board meeting began with the Board thanking George for his four years of service as school director and concluded with a decision of non-contract renewal with no explanation. George was not totally shocked, but was disappointed as he gave his heart and soul to the betterment of the school during the last four years; however, he did feel an element of relief that his future with the school was known. The school year concluded with no negative incidents of note, in fact, George was never asked why he was leaving. It seemed to him that the school-community had already felt satisfied that it knew the full story, at least the story they wanted to believe. George parted ways to later assume another international school directorship.

Literature Review

Leading a school is a daunting task in itself when all key school players are cooperative and follow school policies and procedures. "Relevant, concise, and clear policies are the foundation on which competent and effective leadership rests" (Rebore, 2014, p. 164). They are critical to fulfilling the ultimate goal of a school system, which is to educate all children. School leaders must ascertain that all school community members flourish in a nurturing and safe environment and always keep in mind that the way an individual behaves within the confines of an educational institution may negatively or positively contribute to the "culture of an organization" (Rebore, 2014, p. 57).

Wimpleberg, Teddlie, and Stringfield (1989) suggested that research on successful principal leadership must not only address general characteristics of behavior, such as one's vision, but must also address specific actions, which positively influence student achievement. Waters and Cameron (2007) identified twenty-one specific leadership behaviors related to positive principal leadership. Although good leaders routinely exemplify all or most of the twenty-one leadership behaviors; it is possible for successful leaders to implement only the following four and promote a successful school environment:

1. Fosters shared beliefs and a sense of community and cooperation.
2. Establishes a set of standard operating procedures and routines.
3. Advocate and spokesperson for the school to all stakeholders.

4. Aware of the details and undercurrents in the running of the school and uses this information to address current and potential problems. (pp. 42-43)

Bureaucratic Theory

Bureaucratic theory mentions that if conflict is occurring within an organization, then the organization is experiencing a "breakdown in the organization; failure on the part of management to plan adequately or to exercise sufficient control" (Owens & Valesky, 2011, p. 260). Schools historically continue to be structured and managed bureaucratic entities (Owens & Valesky, 2011; Rebore, 2014), and therefore, are subject to conflict related matters.

Kimbrough and Todd (1967) suggested that the school as a bureaucratic organization does have distractors in the educational community. Advocates for bureaucracy argue that the faults typically associated with bureaucratic organizations can be placed with mismanagement of the organization rather than the qualities inherent within the organization.

Instead of actually being undemocratic, bureaucracy is presented as a form of democracy that enables educators to organize for goal fulfillment to meet the educational needs of the school district. Advocates suggest that leadership within a bureaucratic organization is position oriented (hierarchical) and because of such, minority cliques have little decision-making authority and are more likely to be controlled. Critics of a bureaucratic system have failed to offer a viable alternative to the bureaucratic organization that offers orderly, efficient, educational change.

The type of leadership behavior that is being utilized and how effectively a school is structured are two of several determining factors related to maintaining a successful school environment. The type of leadership and how it is delivered is a key factor in whether or not a school community will have the ability to strive to reach and maintain its goals. Although leaders may be challenged throughout their tenure, it is the soundness of their leadership skills which will ultimately determine whether or not they are effective leaders.

THE GUIDING QUESTIONS

The following questions are intended to stimulate class discussion among educational leadership individuals (novices and practitioners), specifically, those who are current school administrators (director, principal, and assistant principal) and/or those who are in the process of becoming school administrators (director, principal, and assistant principal). The challenges of effectively leading a school through difficult situations are discussed.

Quality of Supervision

1. George may have benefited from conducting a more thorough reference check on Sam, before offering him the position.

    a. What type of information, covered in a reference check, would have been more helpful for George gaining more knowledge regarding Sam's history of the type of behavior exhibited in this case study?
    b. What questions might you consider asking, which would be beneficial in determining a pattern of unacceptable behaviors when vetting an employee?

2. Sam's refusal to follow directives and his behavior exhibiting no regard for students' safety may be classified as exhibiting unprofessional behavior(s).

    a. Does being unprofessional warrant termination?
    b. Was Sam's behavior of an unethical nature or simply, unprofessional?

3. Maintaining a safe school environment is a part of a school director's duties. When parents send their children to school, they expect their children to be safe. Sam's noncompliance regarding the implementation of prescribed school safety measures was not conducive to promoting positive student experiences.

    a. As Sam's primary supervisor, what supervisory strategies and resources would you employ to assist Sam with curtailing his unsafe school environment practices?
    b. List five strategies and five resources readily available to a school leader to assist Sam with promoting a safe environment.

4. As the director of the school, George was obligated to report insubordinate behavior activity to the Board.

    a. What avenues could have he exhausted prior to presenting Sam's situation to the Board?
    b. Discuss what, if any, strategic actions could have been taken prior to presenting the situation to the Board.

Ethical Dilemmas Involving Teachers' Professional Behavior

1. One can argue that George could have prepared the school community for what was going to transpire in regards to terminating the athletic/activities director.

    a. Was he "between the rock and a hard place" in this regard?
    b. What do you think the faculty as a whole felt about the situation playing out before them?

2. As the school director, George is responsible for keeping his school community informed about pressing school matters.

    a. What could George have done to de-escalate the confrontational situation between PTA officers/members who met with him in his office?
    b. Would you recommend meeting with them at a later date? How would you handle the situation?
    c. Ethically, how much information should a school leader divulge about personnel issues?

Due Process and Termination Issues

1. Every employee is subject to termination.

    a. Keeping this in mind, was Sam shown sufficient due process by the Board of Directors, throughout the extenuating circumstances leading to his eventual termination?
    b. Should the Board of Directors have followed a specific protocol when deciding to terminate Sam?
    c. Does a specific termination protocol exist in your educational institution?
    d. Describe what steps an ethical termination process should encompass.

2. The Board ordered Sam's termination before the end of the school year.

    a. Was terminating Sam an ethical and justified action on their part—why or why not?
    b. What contributing factors do you reason caused the untimely termination of this particular school employee?

School Director's Actions

1. Given the volatile circumstances, George went on vacation, regardless of the present situation occurring on campus.

    a. Would you recommend a school leader to take a vacation, when current circumstances at his school were unstable?
    b. As a school community member, how would you describe George's behavior, considerate or selfish? Why?

2. George experienced several important lessons during his tenure as school director.

    a. What specific lessons, positive and/or negative, do you think George learned from his tenure as school director?
    b. What do you consider to be the one most impactful positive and the one most negative learning experience George should reap from this situation? Why?

FINAL CONSIDERATIONS

Final considerations to the questions mentioned above are displayed below. When answering the questions mentioned above, it is necessary to take into account solutions deemed appropriate and ethically sound at your individual educational institution. Consider the following:

1. Many schools' reference checks follow a standard format and do not lend themselves to unique circumstances. How thorough is your school's reference check? Is there room for improvement? Does it assist with vetting an employee?
2. As an effective school administrator it is imperative that you make all of your staff aware of acceptable employee practices. What does your Professional Handbook and the Teacher's Code of Ethics Handbook mention regarding following directives? Are teachers aware of the content found in these handbooks?
3. Maintaining a safe and nurturing school environment is tantamount to establishing a climate of unimpeded learning. How does your school administrator make campus safety a top priority?
4. As a school administrator it is important you exhaust all avenues, prior to reporting insubordinate behavior to your immediate supervisors. What steps does your school have in place to assist administrators with handling insubordinate faculty?

5. As a school administrator it is your responsibility to terminate faculty who are noncompliant with a school's rules and policies, without school community input. How does your school deal with terminating "highly popular" teachers? Should the school community's voice impact an administrators' final decision?
6. A school's PTA may be quite influential in a particular school community. How does your school administrator keep its PTA informed about crucial school matters? What type of information should a school administrator share with its PTA?
7. The termination of a faculty member must be voted on and approved by the School Board. Does your School Board voice their opinion on every recommendation for termination? Do only the "high profile" recommended terminations warrant discussion by the School Board?
8. A School Board, upon reviewing a recommendation for termination, may vote to terminate an employee immediately. What type of circumstances would warrant an immediate termination at your educational institution?
9. As a school administrator, you are always in the public eye. Although the school community cannot dictate when you should and should not take a vacation, it is good practice not to do so when your school is undergoing volatile events.
10. What would you advise George about taking a trip during difficult times?
11. As the school director, George learned many important lessons. How has George's situation affected your own outlook on school administration? After reading this case study, do you believe you will use better judgment when dealing with difficult personnel issues?

REFERENCES

Advisory Board and the Association of American Teachers. (2015). Code of ethics for educators. Retrieved from http://aaeteachers.org/index.php/about-us/aae-code-of-ethics

Boon, H. (2011). Raising the bar: Ethics education for quality teachers. *Australian Journal of Teacher Education, 36*(7), 76-93.

Bolman, L. G., & Deal, T. E. (2008). *Reframing organizations: Artistry, choice, and leadership*. San Francisco, CA: Josey-Bass.

Glickman, C. D., Gordon, S. P., & Ross-Gordon, J. M. (2007). *Supervision and instructional leadership: A developmental approach* (7th ed.). Boston, MA: Pearson Education, Inc.

Gorton, R., & Alston, J. A. (2012). *School leadership and administration: Important concepts, case studies, and simulations* (9th ed.). New York, NY: McGraw-Hill.

Kimbrough, R. B., & Todd, E. A. (1967). Bureaucratic organization and educational change. *Education Leadership, 25*(12), 220-222.

Owens, R. G., & Valesky, T. C. (2011). *Organizational behavior in education: Leadership and school reform* (10th ed.). Boston: Pearson Education.

Smith, E. S. (2008). *Human resources administration: A school based perspective* (4th ed.). London: Routledge.

Rebore, R. W. (2013). *The ethics of educational leadership* (2nd ed.). Upper Saddle River, NJ: Pearson Education.
Rebore, R. W. (2011). *Human resources administration in education* (10th ed.). Upper Saddle River, NJ: Pearson Education.

Chapter Five

The Teacher and the Second Job

Laura Trujillo-Jenks and Rebecca Ratliff Fredrickson

Teachers who are new to the profession are usually excited and enthusiastic about working with children and getting to deliver instruction. Some find the need to supplement their teaching salary with a second position. This concept is not foreign to school districts, but some do have policies that outline what is acceptable as dual employment. The case study that follows concerns a new teacher who has a second job and who unwittingly doesn't follow district policy. The new teacher's lack of knowledge about the dual employment policy gets her in a mess.

THE CASE STUDY

The First Year Teacher

It is the week before school starts, and Ms. Susan Baker is so excited to teach at Pioneer West Middle School in the Pioneer West School District because this is her first teaching job. She will be one of the youngest teachers on the staff, and at 22, she cannot wait to show everyone what an asset she will be for the campus. She has been assigned to teach 7th grade history, and she was asked by her principal to be the cheerleading coach.

Susan came to love teaching after working during a summer with young children at a summer camp for gifted and talented students. She wanted to make a difference in the lives of children, and she enjoyed working with pre-teens because she believed that they could still be molded into good citizens of the world. Her love of children also came from helping her parents raise eight brothers and sisters, and since Susan was the oldest in her family, she learned to love the tasks that came with helping shape the character of each sibling. She knew a job working with children was going to be her destiny, so what better way than to teach?

Although Susan loved her new job, she also knew that teaching was not going to earn her enough money to pay all of her bills, and she needed to find another job soon. One of her close friends, Darla, also needed money and because she was still working on her degree in premedicine, she decided she needed to find a job that earned her fast money.

Darla decided that stripping would be the best and fastest way to earn money, so she gained employment at The Dolls Gentlemen's Club where she worked three nights a week making around $3,000-$5,000 a night. When Susan heard about Darla's fast money, she was skeptical because she could never strip for cash, but she did wait tables in college, and she learned how to bartend. With that, Darla convinced Susan to come with her to work one night and after speaking to the manager, Susan was hired as a new bartender at The Dolls Gentlemen's Club.

Susan didn't think that the bartending job would interfere with her teaching duties because she would only work at night. Bartending at The Dolls was lucrative and Susan made between $1,000-$3,000 from Friday night through Sunday night. Because she was the cheer coach, she was not going to be able to work every weekend, since her girls would be cheering at different events throughout the school year, sometimes on the weekends. No matter what, Susan really felt that since she was not stripping, the bartending job would be okay and that if anyone found out, it should not be devastating or be a conflict of interest with her teaching job. She just hoped no one would find out because the money was too good!

Missed Meeting

The first faculty meeting of the year was a last-minute meeting because the principal was going out of town to see her family due to the death of her father. Because of this rushed beginning of the year, the principal, Mrs. Deal, needed to meet with her teachers before school started next week and before she headed to her family. Therefore, a faculty meeting was called, but not all teachers were present, specifically Susan, who was at a Pioneer West School District mandated new teacher orientation across town. Mrs. Deal asked that all team leaders get with those teachers who missed the meeting and debrief them on the details of the meeting.

At the faculty meeting, the following was discussed:

- A duty roster was handed to each teacher, with an explanation of expectations on where each teacher needed to be on duty during the first week of school.

- An appraisal/evaluation calendar was given to each teacher. Each teacher was informed of which administrator would complete his/her annual evaluation and an annual review of the evaluation standards was conducted.
- Class schedules with class lists were handed out.
- Class Teacher Edition books, materials, and goodie bags were distributed.
- A quick review of the student code of conduct was given.
- Campus safety backpacks were handed out and an explanation and schedule of the different safety drills that would be practiced throughout the year was given.
- The Employment Handbook was discussed and several sections were discussed and highlighted.
- Dual employment requests were explained and documents were distributed to everyone that had a second job. They were told to complete this form. (See Figure 5.1.)

The principal also explained that the dual employment contract needed to be in her office before school started and that anyone who neglected to inform administration about his/her dual employment in a timely manner could be terminated from his/her current position.

Susan did not get back to campus until three days after the faculty meeting was held. Her team leader, who also served as Susan's mentor, reviewed everything she could remember from all of the faculty, department, and team meetings, highlighting what she thought was most important for Susan to understand right away. Hence, the dual employment information was not mentioned.

The Night Out

The school year started off better than expected, and Susan was really grateful in choosing the teaching profession. She worked with a great team and she liked her campus colleagues, overall. Although she wished she had a "real" mentor, one who actually mentored her on how to survive the first year of teaching, she was able to get all of her questions answered by her teammates. She often thought even though she did not make much money, she was luckier than some of her friends in other professions, because she actually went home happy each afternoon and excited to return the next day. Even the cheerleading duties could not curb her enthusiasm, and as she predicted, her second job was an easy one to keep from interfering with her teaching duties.

As Susan prepared to leave work early on a Friday afternoon, a rare treat only occurring due to a football game being cancelled due to the weather, a conversation among a group of male and female teachers in the 8th grade hall was overheard. The 8th grade teachers were about to leave school to celebrate

PIONEER WEST SCHOOL DISTRICT'S
DUAL EMPLOYMENT APPROVAL FORM

Name_____ Date of request_____

Email_____ Cell phone:_____

Employee ID_____ SS#_____

Present school/building employed_____

Current position_____

Primary work schedule--Indicate daily time schedule:

Mon_____ Tues_____ Wed_____ Thurs_____ Fri_____ Sat_____ Sun_____

ADDITIONAL EMPLOYMENT REQUEST

Name of secondary employer_____

First day of second employment_____

Projected last day of employment_____

Reason for second employment_____

Brief description of duties to be performed
_____
_____

Secondary Work Schedule--Indicate daily time schedule:

Mon_____ Tues_____ Wed_____ Thurs_____ Fri_____ Sat_____ Sun_____

I certify that this requested dual employment will not impede on the requirements of my current position and that it will not interfere with the duties assigned to my position.

_____   _____   _____
Printed Name   Signed Name   Date

More explanation on dual employment can be found in the employee handbook on page 15, section 7.3.

Figure 5.1. Pioneer West School District's Duel Employment Approval Form

one team member's upcoming nuptials. At the same time, the strip club that Susan worked at called and asked if Susan could come in and work since one of the bartenders had to stay home with a sick child. Susan readily accepted and left the school.

Later that night, Susan was behind the bar and engrossed in preparing drinks and talking to patrons when two 8th grade teachers from her school saw her and called her over. The two teachers excitedly explained that they were at the strip club celebrating a night out with their groom-to-be teammate and they were excited to see her working. No real conversation occurred except to acknowledge each other's presence and to order drinks.

As Susan watched her colleagues walk back to their table, she noticed that the principal was with them. She thought that it sure was neat to see the leader of her campus spending time with teachers outside of the school day. She had a newfound perspective for Mrs. Deal as she watched her principal putting dollar bills in a stripper's G-string and getting inebriated.

When the 8th grade teachers left with Mrs. Deal, they all were laughing and it was clear that most of them were intoxicated and behaving a bit embarrassingly. Two of the teachers were yelling, "This is the night, this is the night!" Another two teachers were laughing raucously and Mrs. Deal was kissing a stripper on the mouth as the last teacher in the group was tugging at her. Susan was happy to see that her colleagues were having fun, but thought that the leader of her school should not be so brazenly drunk and disorderly.

The Fallout

The following Monday, Susan was in her class during her afternoon conference period when Mrs. Deal walked in with the assistant principal. They both wanted to talk with her about her second job and cited the *Teacher's Code of Ethics*, which stated:

> Standard 3. All educators must behave becoming of an educator with good moral behavior and worthy to carry out all assigned duties, which include working with young children and adults.

They also cited the *Pioneer West School District Employee Handbook*, which stated:

> Section 1.7 Dual Employment—All personnel must disclose their dual employment before the first day of instruction each school year, or within 10 school days from the start date of the dual employment. A dual employment form titled, PIONEER WEST SCHOOL DISTRICT'S DUAL EMPLOYMENT APPROVAL FORM, must be filled out and filed in your campus principal's office before the first day of instruction or by the 10 th day of the dual employment.

As Mrs. Deal began to speak, she came across as disappointed and a bit sarcastic. She stated that she checked the file she had for Susan and found no dual employment form showing that she works at a strip club. Further, Mrs. Deal told Susan that as she learned about Susan's dual employment in a questionable place, she felt ashamed and sick to know that one of her teachers that teaches young minds is also affiliated with a club where strippers and undesirables frequent. The assistant principal just sat back to witness the exchange.

Susan was taken aback and was not sure if the principal was joking around or was serious. As the meeting continued, Susan tried to speak on her behalf, but Mrs. Deal did not allow her to speak. Instead, Mrs. Deal handed her a termination form to sign, which stated in part,

> *Due to your failure to disclose dual employment and due to the violation of the Teacher's Code of Ethics, Standard 3, it has been determined that your employment at Pioneer West School District will cease as of end of day, today.*

When Susan stated that she would like to think about everything that was said during the meeting, Mrs. Deal firmly said that the form needed to be signed immediately so that she could file it with the district office. Susan tried to speak up again, but Mrs. Deal shouted, "Sign the damn form!" Susan reluctantly signed and Mrs. Deal said that Susan would be escorted out of the building at the end of the day. When Susan asked about all of her personal and educational belongings throughout the room, Mrs. Deal said that Susan would be able to pack her stuff over the weekend with the assistant principal supervising. Mrs. Deal and the assistant principal then stood up and walked out of the room. Susan sat stunned and not knowing what to do next, she began to cry.

THE LITERATURE REVIEW

This literature review will focus on the main themes of the case study, which include the knowledge and importance of mentoring first year teachers, understanding the Educator Code of Ethics, and the laws regarding dual employment.

Mentorship

Much of the research on new teachers focuses on their response to entering the world of high-stakes testing but less about how to work with a mentor and find guidance as first year teachers (Neuman, Jones, & Webb, 2012). Due to this, many first year teachers leave the profession within the first five years (Brown, Bay-Borelli, & Scott, 2015; Guarino, Santibanez, & Daley, 2006). New teachers need guidance and must have a seasoned colleague to work with in order to survive the first year. This seasoned colleague should be someone who is invested in the new teacher and is focused on supporting and facilitating the novice's growth. This mentoring partnership, of course, should also be supported and facilitated by the school leadership.

A mentoring partnership is one where both partners, the new teacher and the seasoned teacher, are seen as equal contributors in the mentoring process. The novice, although new to the profession and to the campus, is also teeming with current knowledge, research, and ideas on how to make teaching and learning relevant to students. The mentor, a person who is seen as a master of teaching and learning, understands what it means to be new and appreciates learning from a new teacher as much as teaching and guiding a new teacher. Hence, the mentoring partnership can end up being a win-win, collaborative, learning experience for both partners.

Overall, new teachers have little to no mentoring or induction to assist them with navigating the practical experiences of being a teacher during their first year on the job; if they are lucky enough to have a mentor, the quality and type of that mentoring can vary greatly from school to school (McMahan & Fredrickson, 2012; Ingersol, 2012). Good mentoring can make the difference between teachers staying in the field or leaving within the first five years. In a comprehensive examination of data surrounding the importance of mentoring of first year teachers, Ingersol (2012) noted that,

> Induction has a positive effect...beginning teachers who participated in some kind of induction performed better at...teaching, such as keeping students on task, developing workable lesson plans, using effective student questioning practices, adjusting classroom activities to meet students' interests,...and demonstrating successful classroom management. (p. 51)

Because it has been found that there are positive aspects that can be seen within the classroom when a mentoring or induction program is put in place, it can be safe to assume that a mentor could also help a new teacher understand the policies, rules, and expectations of a school district. This knowledge about these policies, rules, and expectations can help a new teacher "stay out of trouble" and learn the accepted mores of the school district community.

Teacher Code of Ethics

First year teachers are often left to their own devices to determine what the correct thing is to do in many situations and they are often unaware that an Educator's Code of Ethics exists. Most states do have their own concepts or ideas of an Educator Code of Ethics but there is not a "standard" that all follow. Even those that are written are often very vague and broad in scope. In an article by Mukherjee and Rath (2016), they listed what a teacher must be. Some of these concepts include:

Professional ethics are essential to become a good teacher. A teacher is the most accountable and responsible person of the society...The teacher is the architect of a harmonious society...So, a teacher should carry out the expectations of home, society, community and nation. (p. 66)

While this is an admirable listing of what a teacher should be, it is not quantifiable. In the United States, the National Education Association (NEA), which is an educational union, has put forward their concept of an Educator Code of Ethics, which was adopted in 1975. There are two principles that are addressed in the NEA Code of Ethics. These include the commitment to the student and to the profession.

PRINCIPLE I
Commitment to the Student
The educator strives to help each student realize his or her potential as a worthy and effective member of society. The educator therefore works to stimulate the spirit of inquiry, the acquisition of knowledge and understanding, and the thoughtful formulation of worthy goals.
In fulfillment of the obligation to the student, the educator—

1. Shall not unreasonably restrain the student from independent action in the pursuit of learning.
2. Shall not unreasonably deny the student's access to varying points of view.
3. Shall not deliberately suppress or distort subject matter relevant to the student's progress.
4. Shall make reasonable effort to protect the student from conditions harmful to learning or to health and safety.
5. Shall not intentionally expose the student to embarrassment or disparagement.
6. Shall not on the basis of race, color, creed, sex, national origin, marital status, political or religious beliefs, family, social or cultural background, or sexual orientation, unfairly—

    a. Exclude any student from participation in any program
    b. Deny benefits to any student
    c. Grant any advantage to any student

7. Shall not use professional relationships with students for private advantage.
8. Shall not disclose information about students obtained in the course of professional service unless disclosure serves a compelling professional purpose or is required by law.

PRINCIPLE II
Commitment to the Profession
The education profession is vested by the public with a trust and responsibility requiring the highest ideals of professional service.

In the belief that the quality of the services of the education profession directly influences the nation and its citizens, the educator shall exert every effort to raise professional standards, to promote a climate that encourages the exercise of professional judgment, to achieve conditions that attract persons worthy of the trust to careers in education, and to assist in preventing the practice of the profession by unqualified persons.
In fulfillment of the obligation to the profession, the educator—

1. Shall not in an application for a professional position deliberately make a false statement or fail to disclose a material fact related to competency and qualifications.
2. Shall not misrepresent his/her professional qualifications.
3. Shall not assist any entry into the profession of a person known to be unqualified in respect to character, education, or other relevant attribute.
4. Shall not knowingly make a false statement concerning the qualifications of a candidate for a professional position.
5. Shall not assist a noneducator in the unauthorized practice of teaching.
6. Shall not disclose information about colleagues obtained in the course of professional service unless disclosure serves a compelling professional purpose or is required by law.
7. Shall not knowingly make false or malicious statements about a colleague.
8. Shall not accept any gratuity, gift, or favor that might impair or appear to influence professional decisions or action.

Although many of these are quantifiable, it can be difficult to enforce. Most of these statements are also vague and can be difficult to understand, especially for the novice teacher.

Regardless, many states and school districts do employ the Educator Code of Ethics and the language can be seen within school contracts and employee handbooks. Further, the code is seen as sacred and may be received in conjunction with a teaching certificate; it serves as a reminder of how the educator must behave when interacting with students, parents, and colleagues (Trujillo-Jenks & Jenks, 2015).

Dual Employment

Dual employment may also be something that beginning teachers may not understand. These employment policies are made and enforced on a district-by-district basis and may outline what type of dual employment is acceptable. Most school districts don't worry about their employees having another job outside of school hours, as long as their school duties and responsibilities are not shafted or ignored. Additionally, dual employment is seen as a privacy issue and if it doesn't legally interfere with the school district business (i.e., bids on services), then some school districts do not feel it necessary to know about what employees do outside of school hours.

As first year teachers often receive low wages as educators and are paying off student loans, many feel the need to take a second job or "moonlight" just to make ends meet. In an article in the *U.S. News and World Report,* it was stated that across the United States, approximately 10% of teachers have a second job (Bidwell, 2014). In a different report, the National Center for Education Statistics shows that 22% of secondary teachers and 24% of elementary teachers work multiple jobs (Sparks, 2012). This can vary state by state. For example, in Texas 41% of teachers had a second job and 72% had second jobs in North Carolina (Clawson, 2011).

Novice teachers are under great pressure to be experts in their field immediately upon graduation. Added to that pressure are often financial issues that put additional constraints on teachers. As school districts are being held to higher and higher standards, the burden of these improvements falls to teachers where they are asked to work longer hours with no additional compensation. Doing what is best for a school sometimes comes in competition with doing what is best for a teacher to survive financially. Hence, increasing teacher wages or implementing dual employment policies that allow for the possibility of financial freedom may be a conversation that school boards must consider.

THE GUIDING QUESTIONS

The following questions are presented to help you think critically about the case study. Answer them by using your own codes, policies, and laws.

1. First year teachers do not know what they do not know. In order to help first year teachers become successful and to help them master their craft, it is important that administration and team leaders follow up with them. How could this case study fiasco have been prevented? What would you have done differently if you were the team leader? If you were the principal or other campus administrator? What type of mentoring program is present in your school or school district? If none is present, create a policy that addresses a mentoring program.
2. The Educator Code of Ethics is the law that governs how educators must behave. Look up your Educator Code of Ethics. What does it say about dual employment? About teachers working in questionable environments? Is there anything in your school district policies that address dual employment? If so, following your handbook, how would you have addressed the teacher in this case? Do you feel that Susan was employed in a questionable job since she was not stripping? Support your response from your Educator Code of Ethics, employee

handbook, or any other evidence that you can find within your school district or state.
3. As an administrator, it may be necessary to terminate a teacher within your school for multiple reasons. Moral turpitude is just one example of this. According to your school district policy, how does an administrator go about terminating a teacher's contract? What state policies support this action? Do you feel that Susan should be terminated? If so, what evidence would you use to support this? If not, what measures do you feel should be taken?

FINAL CONSIDERATIONS

Some final considerations to the problems above are listed below. Finding the right solution is based on finding the right supporting evidence. As you work through each question above, reflect on the following considerations. For question 1, there are multiple ways that this fiasco could have been prevented. For starters, administrators should take note to

- not present information to teachers while new teachers are out of the room doing new teacher orientation;
- work with the new teachers to understand the district policies;
- assign the new teacher a mentor to assist them and check up on them throughout the year; and
- discuss personal and personnel matters privately and give due process to the teacher and the opportunity for her to quit her second job.

Whatever is decided as far as what could be done differently, be sure that it is grounded in policy, or code. You want to be able to support what you are doing with evidence that cannot be disputed. Using the language of a policy, law, or code helps keep you legal and honest. And, no matter how mentoring is done in your district, as a teacher leader or administrator, focus on what a first year teacher needs in order to be successful on your campus and in your district. Also, reflect on what would have made you more successful in your first year.

For question 2, concerning the code of ethics, various states have different sets of standards defining ethics. As you are examining yours, consider what it says (or does not say) about educators working in questionable environments. Does it define what would be a questionable environment? Is dual employment even addressed? If it is, how is it addressed and defined? In the *Sunnydale School District Employee Handbook*, dual employment is addressed in one sentence. How does this compare to your handbook? Is this enough?

Additionally, when understanding the code of ethics, it is necessary to understand how "questionable," moral turpitude, or any other word used to encompass immoral or unethical actions by a district employee is defined by the School Board. If the School Board has not given clear definitions on what is acceptable or not acceptable dual employment, can a teacher be justifiably terminated? Due process is something that must be given to all persons on a campus. Has Mrs. Deal given due process to Susan? How do you prove that due process has been given or not?

When addressing the third question, does your school district have a "morals clause" in teacher contracts? In many contracts or policies the moral turpitude clause is often too vague for it be enforceable. However, supportive evidence helps administrators enforce policies and helps an administrator have credibility, especially when having to terminate a teacher's contract. What supportive evidence that clearly violates the dual employment clause did Mrs. Deal show Susan?

No matter if you believe if there is enough evidence or not, it is important to be sure that you keep your biases at bay. It does not matter what second job a teacher has; that job is one fact or supportive evidence in the equation. All that matters is what policy is being violated? Is there enough evidence to terminate Susan's contract; based on what violations? The measures that should be taken must align with the expectations set forth by the School Board and state law. Therefore, it should be easy to keep your biases out of the equation.

REFERENCES

Bidwell, A. (2014). Many teachers rely on second jobs. *U.S. News and World Report.* Retrieved from: http://www.usnews.com/news/blogs/data-mine/2014/07/23/more-than-1-in-10-american-teachers-rely-on-second-jobs

Brown, C. P., Bay-Borelli, D.E., & Scott, J. (2015). Figuring out how to be a teacher in a high-stakes context? A case study of first-year teachers' conceptual and practical development. *Action in Teacher Education, 37*(1), 45-64.

Clawson, L. (2011). Low pay leads 20% of teachers to work second jobs. Retrieved from: http://www.dailykos.com/story/2011/11/11/1035496/-

Guarino, C. M., Santibanez, L., & Daley, G. (2006). Teacher recruitment and retention: a review of the recent empirical literature. *Review of Educational Research, 76,* 173-208.

Ingersol, R.M. (2012) Beginning teacher induction: What the data tell us. *Phi Delta Kappan, 93*(8), 47-51.

McMahan, S., & Fredrickson, R. R. (2012). *The impact of mentoring relationships between faculty members and preservice teacher education candidates.* Proceedings of the University of New Mexico Annual Mentoring Conference, Albuquerque, NM.

Mukherjee, C., & Rath, J. P. (2016). Professional ethics: A prerequisite in teaching profession. *Indian Journal of Applied Research, 6*(2), 66-69.

NEA Handbook, 1977-1978. Washington, DC: National Education Association. Retrieved from: http://www.nea.org/home/30442.htm

Neumann, M., Jones, L. C., & Webb, P. T. (2012). Claiming the political: The forgotten terrain of teacher leadership knowledge. *Action in Teacher Education, 34,* 2-13.

Sparks, S.D. (2012). Federal data show teacher more likely to juggle multiple jobs. *Education Week*. Retrieved from: http://blogs.edweek.org/edweek/inside-school-research/2012/11/ed_data_shows_teachers_more_li.html

Trujillo-Jenks, L., & Jenks, K. (2015). *Case studies on safety, bullying, and social media in schools: Current issues in educational leadership.* New York, NY: Routledge Publishers.

Chapter Six

Innovation and State Testing

The Challenges of a University Charter School

Wesley D. Hickey and Joanna Neel

University administrators have become more progressive during the past decade, in part due to increased financial constraints, and in part to be more influential. One consideration for administrators is to create a university charter school for primary and secondary students. Adding a charter to the university provides the potential for a pipeline of students, and it can become a laboratory for innovative educational practices. However, there are growing pains with any endeavor, and the creation of the charter school in this case study, University Charter, is no exception.

Within the case study, "application boxes" (represented as tables) related to educational concepts that were issues or strategies within University Charter can be found. The purpose of these activities is to give the student an opportunity to develop skills that will refine his or her professional repertoire.

THE CASE STUDY

University Charter, in fulfilling its mission to be innovative, chose to use project-based learning (PBL) as the fundamental method of imparting problem solving and critical thinking within the curriculum. Everything about PBL and University Charter was to be student driven. Students were to decide within each project what needed to be known and how to accomplish meeting that need. The teacher's role was to present opportunities for authentic learning and intervene only as students needed assistance. Theoretically,

PBL would provide the foundation for increasing student achievement in all areas, including state standardized tests.

"Life is PBL." was a common belief among the leadership team for University Charter. Every new learning experience, challenge or problem encountered in everyday life was considered a form of PBL project. Students who worked in a PBL environment were not to be simply completing assignments but living. This belief that educational projects and life lessons should correlate was core to how University Charter planned to utilize PBL. The steps in the learning process included the development of the required standards, increasing the student's understanding, and experiencing authentic real-world experiences. One of these real-world experiences was interacting with technology.

Using technology in University Charter had several benefits to students that extend beyond the development of computer skills. Technology can be a one-to-one teacher for students, as engagement and achievement are highly correlated. A student who is sitting in a classroom listening to a lecture may be present but not engaged, so initiatives that promoted increased time on task would be beneficial. A student must work the assignment and complete an accountability measure to get credit and move forward with the curriculum. The computer provided the presentation of material and allowed for original learning in total engagement. This was supposed to provide a baseline of student understanding for assessment purposes.

The effectiveness of this engagement could be determined through diagnostic tests as a part of the accountability measures. Technology easily provided questions to ensure mastery of the curriculum and has the capability of addressing deficiencies through proper placement within the discipline. Gaps in knowledge can lead to further difficulties, thus, immediate remediation helps to ensure a proper foundation for future learning.

Application #1
You are a first year teacher who just provided an assessment to students in order to measure their understanding of a standard. Overall, 80% of the students did well. Provide a list of 5 remediation activities for the 20% of students who did not meet expectations. These activities should use technology or be embedded within a PBL assignment.

Technology can further enhance the learning process by providing the tools for professional products. Students, in developing projects, can increase the quality of work. The potential that technology presents for increased quality should result in higher expectations for student performance.

A final characteristic of technology that was valued was the ability to communicate quickly with parents. There are the old-school communication methods of email, Facebook, and Twitter, but the information that is most important is making student work available to parents. Electronic blogs provide this mechanism, allowing parents to see what their child is doing. The more the parent is involved, the better a child will perform. Utilizing e-blogs provides immediate feedback to students from multiple sources. These discussions add to the engagement that is related to learning.

Application #2
There are different blogs on the Internet that will allow students to upload work and share with parents. One is Edublogs (edublogs.org). Create an account and share your methods of remediation (see application #1) on your new blog. Explore ways in which students could use this technology to privately share work with his or her parents.

Successful use of technology is predicated upon two factors. First, the school must have a teaching culture that values creativity and innovation, and second, training must be sufficient to provide educators and students the foundation for success. This means that hiring the right teachers was a vitally important step in the process of University Charter being successful.

There are few aspects of an administrators' job more important than hiring the highest quality teachers that can be found. A successful school starts with high-quality personnel. Historical hiring processes are not always effective in getting the best person for the job, as some candidates are excellent at conveying the traits of creativity, innovation, student-centeredness, collegiality, collaborative nature, self-starter, etc., within an interview, but these characteristics may be absent in posthire performance.

University Charter recognized the importance of hiring the best teachers available, and traditional practices were believed to be ineffective. The instructional leaders of the school created a four-step process that was designed to be both efficient and effective. The steps included

1. The sending of the cover letter/resume and formally applying for the position. This is the process everyone uses for both practical and legal reasons. The pool of candidates that apply to the position(s) are narrowed based upon education, experience, and skills. Savvy candidates would highlight traits and skills related to the needs of University Charter, but this initial process is similar to everyone who hires.
2. A fifteen-minute Skype interview. Candidates chosen from resumes were invited to a remote interview using Skype. This was designed to see how comfortable the candidate was with technology and how he or she utilized the format to create a positive impression. Most individuals have received instruction on dress and interaction in a formal inter-

view, but a Skype interview is different. A successful candidate had to be aware of background, sound, engagement issues, and more. Creativity and technological savvy were at a premium.
3. Invitation to create a short video. The emphasis on technology, creativity, and innovation were emphasized once again. Producing a short video (around 10 minutes) allowed for the demonstration of each one of these traits. In addition, candidates who lacked initiative found this step unreasonable and removed his or her name from consideration. These are individuals who the charter would not want to hire, so this self-eliminating process assisted in getting stronger employees.
4. Face-to-face interview. Candidates who made it past the video presentation were invited to campus for a traditional face-to-face interview. This allowed the selection committee to ask a few more questions in depth and ascertain the level of personal connection that the candidate had in interactions.

The interview process is important for both the school and candidate. There are skills related to interviewing that the candidate needs to be able to perform, and the school is trying to determine whether the candidate can be effective in the school's environment. University Charter needed technologically proficient teachers who had the creativity to lead students on PBL products.

> Application #3
> Create a video of yourself answering the following two interview questions: 1) Describe how you will manage your classroom to promote student learning; and 2) Describe a project that you will use that will have students actively engaged. Upload this video on YouTube (create an account if you do not already have one) and provide the link in your Edublog (developed in application #2).

Year One

The school year started with excitement. The university had a new charter school, an innovative curriculum, and teachers who proved they could use technology and creativity in the classroom. Parents and students were excited about PBL for two reasons:

1. It provided an authentic, engaging learning environment
2. It de-emphasized state standardized tests

Many of the students who transferred into University Charter were from home school environments, and these parents did not like the evolution of instruction that resulted from state testing. Other students were simply struggling academically and were looking for answers. The charter was subject to most of the requirements of public schools, including state testing, so these parents were not getting away from accountability, but they were looking for a more well-rounded philosophy of addressing these mandates.

A charter school with a philosophy of eliminating state test preparation, and parents who agreed, made for an interesting dynamic. The PBL approach was popular among all stakeholders, and parents felt like communication was good. The superintendent continued to de-emphasize the high-stakes tests, so there were no benchmarks and teachers were discouraged from providing any objective measures of competency, relying solely on presentations and products to determine whether the standard was understood.

There were some concerns about this lack of objective practice, but the superintendent told the teachers that taking the tests would work out because it would be viewed as another project. Students were presented with this challenge a couple of weeks before testing. There was excitement as the students determined the best way to approach this test, and the teachers coached them with some strategies.

The University Charter received its scores a few weeks after the test, and the results were dismal. Reading scores were the highest, but they were below the state average, and math scores were toward the low end of the scale. The college dean and university president both asked for a meeting to discuss the test performance, as a charter school connected with the university that did not score well was seen as a liability.

An analysis of the situation suggested that the lack of objective measures did not prepare the students for the state accountability. Authentic learning is not a part of state tests but textual prompts out of context with multiple-choice items were. This is a different skill for students, and it was one in which they were not prepared. Teachers who had worked hard to create an engaging environment that was technology-rich had failed to bridge instruction with the tests in which the students were to be held accountable. There was plenty of blame to go around, but it started with the superintendent who discouraged objective tests. The next year had to be different.

Application #4
Provide a blog entry (created in application #2) discussing how you would ensure student competency on high-stakes testing while providing an active and engaging environment in the classroom.

THE LITERATURE REVIEW

Charter schools have been a political initiative for many years, and the results include some significant failures (Schwenkenberg & VanderHoff, 2015) as well as some great successes (Caserio, 2015). The philosophical issue within the charter school debate has less to do with effectiveness and more to do with choice (Davis & Raymond, 2012). The freedom to make a personal decision regarding the education of one's child has become a patriotic mantra among many politicians, which means that legislation will be passed to further expand opportunities for charter schools, including those within universities.

University charter schools are not new, but few higher education institutions have them. Many states have regulations like Texas, which has a founding document that requires the charter holder to "explain in succinct terms the ways in which the school, if authorized, will differ from the traditional neighborhood schools or charter schools that currently operate in the area where the school or schools would be located" (Texas Administrative Code, 2015). This requirement distinctly states that a university charter school cannot be like everyone else, and this presents a challenge in regard to state testing.

The concept of required state standardized testing as a measure of student and school performance is concerning among many parents and teachers (de Vinck, 2015). The variability of students, the limits of concepts that can be measured on objective tests, and general stress related to the activity have had many parents look for other options (Sanchez, 2015). Schools hear these concerns regularly, and many attempt innovative educational methodologies designed to increase student engagement with authentic work. But authentic work is not measured on standardized tests, and schools who are concerned with state ratings often return to mundane test preparation.

The reason many schools drill students on objective questions in preparation for state tests is that it works. Schools have evolved in the use of this method because it prepares students for the tests in which each one will be held accountable. The current status of public education is the product of legislation of which the campuses strive to be in compliance. This makes a university charter school more interesting; by statute the education is to be different.

Innovative instructional models are of interest because traditional education tends to disenfranchise a large percentage of students. Educators would like to have active, engaged, higher level thinking students who enjoy the experience of education and do well on the standardized tests required by the state and federal government. This is not always easy. Oliveras (2014) correlated teacher evaluations with standardized test scores and found the relationship was weak. In other words, the teachers we recognize as being excellent based upon their classroom evaluations do not always have great test scores.

This potential problem with good teaching has been recognized by Schlechty (2011), who identified quality teaching as designing interesting assignments based upon the desired curriculum. He stated "there is...some empirical evidence to support the inference that teachers who encourage superficial coverage of content are more likely to produce quick results than are teachers who insist on expecting students to be involved more profoundly with the content being tested" (p. 180).

Schlechty (2011) optimistically believes that his model of teaching can be as good on standardized tests as the classroom that mundanely drills students on objective questions, but admits that it takes more work and training. This is something that many schools know, and it is one of the reasons that our schools have evolved as they have. State and federal mandates provide limited uniqueness among schools and uniformity is common (Madaus & Russell, 2010/2011). Technological innovations of the past twenty years have provided new educational possibilities, but most are tweaked to fit the factory model mold. The tools exist for significant educational change (Bramante & Colby, 2012; Christensen, 2011), but few schools are adopting them.

All states have some version of standardized testing (Fletcher, 2009), and there is nothing inherently wrong with it. Testing can provide valuable information for improvement if it is used properly. Problems occur when testing becomes the purpose of schools. These concerns led Texas Commissioner of Education Robert Scott to call the current standardized testing emphasis a "perversion of its original intent" at the 2012 Texas Association of School Administrators Conference in Austin (Strauss, 2012). This perversion is evident in schools that work hard with students until the test dates are complete. The rest of the school year is spent with parties and time wasters, leading an impartial observer to believe the purpose of schools is to take standardized tests.

That decontextualized information introduced to students in a text format are often the default for teachers and tests is disheartening (Au, 2011). This format limits the depth and meaning required for passionate student engagement, and the schoolroom will be the last place these students will use this skill. Most people would argue that schools are to develop students for any future endeavors, and if answering objective tests are not a part this future, it is of limited value. Yet it is the focus of many schools.

There is a place for objective tests but not as the ultimate mission of schools (Ravitch, 2010). A modern school should focus on creativity and problem solving (Zhou, Hirst, & Shipton, 2011). These personal traits are often recognized as important for the economic development of the United States. Furthermore, a modern school needs to take advantage of the technological advances provided by computers, tablets, and software. These allow for both learning and diagnostic tests to assure that students understand the curriculum as they should.

This being said, educators must be pragmatists. There are components of all occupations that seem ill advised, but they must be done. Teachers must provide both an engaging classroom and students prepared for high-stakes testing. This requires consistent instruction that connects the authentic learning to the text format of objective tests. This provides the data for determining competency and whether a student knows the content. And of course, teachers must provide remediation for students who do not understand the standards in the way in which the student will be held accountable. Our schools can be both authentic and practical, but it takes a well-trained and dedicated teacher to make it happen; otherwise, we go back to drill and kill.

THE GUIDING QUESTIONS

1. What type of school would you create if you could start from scratch? What role would active student engagement and technology have in your school?
2. How does your ideal school meet both the needs of the students and mandates from the government?
3. What are skills that will be required of effective teachers in the 21st century? How would these skills be measured in an interview?
4. What are the pros and cons of government high-stakes standardized testing? How would you change these current requirements to better meet student needs?
5. What are some instructional strategies for creating meaningful and engaging classrooms while preparing students high-stakes testing?

FINAL CONSIDERATIONS

The charter school movement has led many well-meaning individuals to start schools, believing that the desire to create an engaging environment for students is enough to have them achieve according to legislative definitions of success. In most states, academic success and scoring well on the high-stakes standardized tests is the same thing. This creates concern among many professional educators, parents, and students, not only because the test is just one component of a great education, but also due to the stress it creates in students, as well as the evolution that occurs in schools in creating increased value on deconstructing objective questions as opposed to working on meaningful activities.

Charter school leaders, in order to be successful with state ratings based upon standardized tests, must have effective strategies to make sure students understand the standards in objective form. Authentic assignments do not always do this.

One way to bridge authentic learning to state tests is to interleave objective questions within the work. This means a student will work on an authentic assignment for awhile, but the teacher creates breaks in activities where students look at a question related to the work in the way in which they will be tested at the end of the year.

There are other ways to do this, only limited by the creativity of great teachers. A great teacher manages to connect instruction in motivational and meaningful ways to the student while aligning with other requirements. There is nothing more important to a school than hiring great teachers. Do this, and most issues are resolved.

Hiring processes in the 21st century allow for video clips, e-portfolios, videoconferences, background checks, and many other clues as to the quality of the applicant. The hiring process should be thorough, but it should avoid being onerous to either the applicant or the hiring committee. The steps in the process should be focused on hiring the best teacher possible, but it should eliminate the unproductive and extraneous.

Creating a school from scratch is difficult, but many are doing it in this day of charter schools. Knowing how to achieve academically according to legislative dictates, while providing a meaningful environment, requires purposeful planning. Start with great teachers, and always bridge to the way in which the student will be held accountable.

REFERENCES

Au, W. (2011). Teaching under the new Taylorism: High-stakes testing and the standardization of the 21st century curriculum. *Journal of Curriculum Studies, 43*(1), 25-45.

Bramante, F., & Colby, R. (2012). *Off the clock: Moving education from time to competency.* Thousand Oaks, CA: Corwin.

Caserio, M. (2015). *The charter school of Wilmington: A case study of the factors influencing development and success* (Unpublished doctoral dissertation). Wilmington University, Wilmington, Delaware.

Christensen, C. M. (2011). *Disrupting class: How disruptive innovation will change the way the world learns.* New York: McGraw Hill.

Davis, D. H., & Raymond, M. E. (2012). Choices for studying choice: Assessing charter school effectiveness using two quasi-experimental methods. *Economics of Education Review, 31*(2), 225-236.

de Vinck, C. (2015). A failing grade for the notion of more testing. *Education Digest, 80*(9), 27-30.

Fletcher, D. (2009, December 11). Standardized testing. *Time.* Retrieved from http://www.time.com/time/nation/article/0,8599,1947019,00.html

Madaus, G., & Russell, M. (2010/2011). Paradoxes of high stakes testing. *Journal of Education, 190*(1/2), 21-30.

Oliveras, Y. (2014). *The empirical relationship between administrator ratings of teacher effectiveness and student achievement on the state of Texas assessments of academic readiness* (Unpublished doctoral dissertation). The Pennsylvania State University, University Park, Pennsylvania.

Ravitch, D. (2010). *The death and life of the great American school system: How testing and choice are undermining education*. New York: Basic Books.

Sanchez, C. (2015). Why some parents are sitting kids out of tests. Retrieved from http://www.npr.org/blogs/ed/2015/03/05/390239788/why-some-parents-are-sitting-kids-out-of-tests

Schlechty, P. C. (2011). *Engaging students: The next level of working on the work*. San Francisco: Jossey-Bass.

Schwenkenberg, J., & VanderHoff, J. (2015). Why do charter schools fail? An analysis of charter school survival in New Jersey. *Contemporary Economic Policy, 33*(2), 300-314.

Sivakumaran, T., Holland, G., & Heyning, K. (2010). Hiring agents' expectations for new teacher portfolios. *National Forum of Teacher Education Journal, 20*(3), 1-6.

Strauss, V. (2012). *Texas schools chief calls testing obsession a "perversion."* Retrieved from http://www.washingtonpost.com/blogs/answer-sheet/post/texas-schools-chief-calls-testing-obsession-a-perversion/2012/02/05/gIQA5FUWvQ_blog.html

Texas Administrative Code. (2015). *Commissioner's Rules Concerning Open-Enrollment Charter Schools*. Retrieved from http://ritter.tea.state.tx.us/rules/tac/chapter100/ch100aa.html

Zhou, Q., Hirst, G., & Shipton, H. (2011). Promoting creativity at work: The role of problem-solving demand. *Applied Psychology, 61*(1), 56-80.

Chapter Seven

Psychosocial Factors Impacting Bullying in a School Context

Responses for Campus Safety

Shannon R. Scott, Kathy DeOrnellas, and Lisa H. Rosen

Bullying is a problem and must be taken seriously when reported. Educators must understand what bullying is so that they may help students work through bullying issues. The following case is about a student who has not found the right educator to help her feel safe at school.

THE CASE STUDY

Hayleigh is a 7th grader who attends a suburban middle school in the northeast. She is an average preteen who comes from a single parent home with an older brother. She spends a lot of time online and tends to be quiet when she first meets a new person. However, once she knows the person, she can be quite talkative. Hayleigh does not have a history of being disruptive in school or at home. Throughout this school year, she has had several negative experiences in school which have never happened to her previously.

Several of Hayleigh's male peers have begun making comments about her physical appearance. They comment on her weight, as well as her hair. They call her a cow and make "mooing" sounds when she walks by. They also talk about her "nappy hair." Hayleigh has begun wearing oversized clothing to hide her body but there is little she can do about her hair since she is not allowed to wear a hat at school. She does her best and practices good hygiene but her family can't afford expensive trips to the salon. Due to these comments, Hayleigh walks through the hallways avoiding eye contact with her head lowered.

In addition, many of her female peers have begun to spread rumors about Hayleigh throughout the school. Even though she has never dated anyone, her peers have labeled her a "slut" and tell everyone that she has been sexually active with many of the boys in her school. They also state that she has said mean things about the popular kids in her school. Her female peers have created a "Hate Hayleigh" Facebook page that has been the source of a lot of hallway chatter at school. They also send mean text messages throughout the school day, as well as all night.

Between the Facebook page and the text messages, Hayleigh is being bombarded with messages from people she doesn't even know about how she should "just kill herself and make the world a better place." The taunts and the name-calling are constant and Hayleigh feels overwhelmed, worthless, and completely alone when at school. She constantly wonders what her classmates are thinking about her and whether they have seen the Facebook page or heard the rumors.

This has escalated to a recent physical altercation. Several girls walked alongside Hayleigh in the hall at school, pulled her hair, and knocked her books out of her hands. When she bent to pick up her books, another female pushed her from behind causing her to fall to the ground. Hayleigh sat on the floor of the hallway crying until the school resource officer noticed students were laughing or taunting her. Officer Stanford yelled, "Knock it off and get to class," made sure everyone had left the area, and then went back to her office. As soon as Hayleigh heard the officer's voice, she grabbed her books and ran.

After the incident, Hayleigh went to her next class where the teacher asked her what was wrong. She complained of feeling sick and the teacher sent her to the nurse's office. The nurse is well acquainted with Hayleigh as she often visits with headaches and stomachaches. She had her lie down in a darkened room for about thirty minutes before sending her to her next class.

Other students had heard the rumors or witnessed Hayleigh being pushed, but chose to just ignore these situations so that they would not become targets themselves. Several of the students have told teachers about the "Hate Hayleigh" page when they were caught looking at Facebook during class. However, the students mostly talk among themselves rather than involving the teachers.

All of Hayleigh's teachers discussed the Facebook page and the altercation in the hallway. There is some disagreement between them as to how the situation should be handled. Although they agree that Hayleigh does not deserve the treatment she is being given, some of the teachers feel it would be better for her if they did not get involved.

Bullying has been a problem at the school for years and it seems that each year a new student is selected to be the victim. In their experience, the bullying will probably stop when the students move on to high school. However, one teacher states that she plans to talk to Hayleigh about standing up for herself.

Hayleigh attends a large middle school and, because she has never been in trouble, her name is not known to her principal. When the teachers inform him of the Hate Hayleigh Facebook page, he remarks that what happens on Facebook is not school business. The teachers remind him that students are accessing Facebook from their phones while at school and this is having an impact on their classes. The principal does not feel that any actions by the school are necessary at this time.

The counselor at Hayleigh's school heard about the altercation in the hallway and called Hayleigh to her office. It was her first time to meet Hayleigh and she found her to be a sad and frightened girl. She was dressed in baggy clothing and had her hair slicked back into a ponytail. The counselor tried to talk to Hayleigh about the bullying but she was afraid to say anything. After several minutes of trying to talk to Hayleigh about bullying in general and getting no response, she sent her back to class. The counselor decided to keep an eye out for additional problems.

Hayleigh's mother, Janice, is very concerned but does not know the source of Hayleigh's problems. Janice has watched her change over the course of the school year. She began the school year quiet but happy and eager to make new friends. Now, she is withdrawn and depressed. Since she will not discuss the bullying at school, Janice turns to Hayleigh's brother for information.

Several years older, Calvin has friends with younger brothers at the middle school. He finds out that Hayleigh is being called names, has been physically assaulted, and is the victim of a malicious Facebook page. He tries talking to Hayleigh about it but she has little to say. Calvin shares this information with their mother. Janice tried to sit down and talk to Hayleigh about the situation but she refused to talk and told her mother to stay out of it because she is afraid Janice will make things worse for her. Janice is trying to decide what to do as the problem seems to be escalating.

The one person Hayleigh confides in is Sally, the program director at the local Boys and Girls Club. Hayleigh has been going to the afterschool program at the Boys and Girls Club since she was in kindergarten and also has attended summer programs for the last seven years. She has developed a strong bond with the staff there. Sally has noticed the changes in Hayleigh and has observed some of the fellow students calling her names. Sally told Hayleigh to ignore her peers and to remember how special she is. She encouraged her to "hang in there as it will get better" and to "believe in herself." Sally has attempted to contact the school but did not receive a response.

THE LITERATURE REVIEW

Researchers began to systematically study school bullying in the 1970s, and the majority of this early work was completed in Scandinavia. More recently, work in this area has surged across the world with growing recognition that school bullying is a public health problem of global concern (Smith, 2011). Bullying can be defined as a subtype of aggressive behavior in which a victim is "exposed, repeatedly and over time, to negative actions on the part of one or more other student" (Olweus, 1993, 9). These negative actions can take many forms, including name calling, spreading rumors, and physical attacks, but in order for a behavior to be considered bullying, the following three conditions must be met:

1. the behavior is carried out with the intention to harm the victim;
2. the behavior recurs over time; and
3. a power imbalance exists with the bully or bullies having greater power than the victim (Nansel et al., 2001).

Bullying is common in schools worldwide. A study that sampled from schools in 40 countries found that approximately 26% of students were involved in bullying with 10.7% of students identified as bullies, 12.6% of students identified as victims, and 3.6% of students identified as bully/victims (Craig et al., 2009). However, it is important to note that there does appear to be substantial cross-cultural variability in the percentage of students who are bullied based on responses to a World Health Organization survey collected from students in 28 countries.

The lowest level of bullying was reported in Sweden where 5.1% of girls and 6.3% of boys reported experiencing bullying, and the highest level of bullying was reported in Lithuania where 38.2% of girls and 41.4% of boys reported experiencing bullying (Due et al., 2005). These cross-cultural differences in prevalence in bullying may be due in part to national policies as countries, such as Sweden have laws in place to protect children and have launched large-scale anti-bullying campaigns. In addition, part of the variability may be due to cultural differences in how bullying is conceptualized and defined.

Although differences exist in the prevalence of bullying across cultures, bullying is consistently associated with myriad forms of maladjustment. Although diverse cultures were examined, a consistent pattern was found with bullying being related to increased physical health concerns and psychological symptoms in each of the 28 countries examined (Due et al. 2005). Children who are bullied are at elevated risk for both internalizing problems (e.g., anxiety and depression) and externalizing problems (e.g., delinquency and substance use; Sullivan, Farrell, & Kliewer 2006).

The association between victimization and maladjustment is found for each form of bullying (e.g., physical bullying, verbal bullying, social/relational bullying, and cyberbullying). Physical bullying is characterized by the victim being subjected to physical maltreatment. Students who are verbally bullied are teased by their peers and called names. In social or relational bullying, a student or students attempt to harm a peer's social status and relationships by engaging in behaviors, such as intentional social exclusion or malicious gossip (Underwood, 2003).

More recently with the growing proliferation of electronic technologies, greater attention is being devoted to cyberbullying, which has been defined as "willful and repeated harm inflicted through the use of computers, cell phones, and other electronic devices" (Hinduja & Patchin, 2009, p. 5). Although bullying takes many forms, students who experience any type of bullying are at increased risk for adjustment problems.

Many bullying incidents take place in the school setting. Students report that 82% of episodes of emotional bullying and 59% of peer assaults happen at school (Turner et al., 2011). Approximately 30% of adolescents experience cyberbullying in the school setting (Feinberg & Robey, 2008). Within the school environment, students report bullying being frequent in the classroom, lunchroom, and hallways (Perkins, Perkins, & Craig, 2001). Given the amount of bullying that occurs in the school setting, it is imperative that teachers and school administrators work together to reduce bullying.

The majority of teachers report feeling responsible to stop bullying in their classrooms (Boulton, 1997). However, teachers are more bothered by physical and verbal bullying and tend to perceive social bullying as less problematic. Based on these beliefs, teachers are less likely to intervene in instances of social bullying (Bauman & Del Rio, 2006). As there are negative consequences associated with experiencing each form of bullying, it is imperative that educators expand their intervention efforts to address social, as well as physical forms of bullying.

There are a number of ways that teachers and other school officials can work to reduce all forms of bullying in their classrooms and campuses (Cassidy, Faucher, & Jackson, 2013). First and foremost, teachers and school officials can help to establish and implement effective policies and practices to combat bullying. This includes developing, assessing, and continuing to revise bullying prevention programs. In addition, psychoeducational programs can be integrated into the curriculum to focus on building social skills and regulatory abilities (Cassidy, Faucher, & Jackson, 2013).

Bullying prevention efforts vary dramatically in their effectiveness. A recent meta-analysis found that school-based bullying prevention and intervention programs can decrease bullying by about 20% (Ttofi & Farrington, 2011). Certain program elements are associated with program efficacy including program intensity, parent involvement, firm discipline strategies, and increased supervision on the playground. Conversely, peer involvement in the program, such as through peer mediation, seems to be detrimental to the success of the program.

One of the most successful programs identified is the Olweus Bullying Prevention Program, and this has served as a model program in North America and Europe (Smith, 2011). This program operates at multiple levels including the school level, classroom level, and individual level incorporating the greater community whenever possible (Olweus & Limber, 2010).

At the school level, the program entails staff training, discussion among staff members, and sessions to introduce the anti-bullying rules. At the classroom level, teachers post the anti-bullying rules and frequently discuss these rules with their students. At the individual level, teachers and administrators meet with those identified as bullies and victims separately and intervene whenever they witness bullying of any form.

Bullying is a significant problem in schools around the world. In addition to the long-standing forms of bullying (e.g., verbal and physical aggression), bullying has become more sophisticated due to ease of access to technology. Students are now able to bully other students from their computers and their cell phones. No matter what type of bullying students are subjected to, they are adversely affected—both emotionally and academically. Since all of these behaviors can take place on the school campus, school personnel are charged with making a campus a safer place for all students. There are a number of anti-bullying programs available but many are of limited effectiveness. The programs that show the most promise are those that involve students, school personnel, parents, and the community.

THE GUIDING QUESTIONS

1. What psychosocial factors might contribute to Hayleigh's situation?
2. As there is an indication that bullying is an ongoing problem at this school, what responsibility do school officials have in creating a safe environment for all students? How might they accomplish this?
3. For each of the following school officials, were their responses appropriate? If not, how might each have been more effective?

    a. Principal
    b. School resource officer

c. Teachers
   d. Counselor
   e. Nurse

4. How can communication between school officials be facilitated?
5. Should (and if so, how) school officials involve Hayleigh's mother in the situation?
6. Should bullying on social media or texting be addressed by school officials? If the school decides to address bullying on social media or texting, how might this be accomplished?
7. What specific recommendations would you give to each of the following individuals:

   a. Hayleigh
   b. Hayleigh's mother and brother
   c. The program director for the Boys and Girls Club

FINAL CONSIDERATIONS

Some final considerations to the problems above are listed below.

1. Consider aspects of Hayleigh and her family situation that may make her vulnerable to being bullied. Consider how identification of these factors could help in this situation, as well as how you would do this without creating an environment in which the victim, Hayleigh, is blamed for the bullying.
2. Consider how school policies, both official and implied, may contribute to or prevent bullying. How might a "bullying" environment be created and sustained?
3. Consider how school personnel's beliefs about their role in stopping bullying influence their behavior toward bullying victims. If they believe bullying is a "rite of passage" for students, how might this influence their behaviors? Consider the different roles of each individual and how these roles may lead to different types of or levels of involvement in the prevention of bullying.
4. Keeping in mind that school personnel are very busy with teaching, high-stakes testing, and more severe behavior problems, how important is it for school personnel to communicate with each other regarding bullying? What policies or procedures may best facilitate this communication?
5. Hayleigh has expressed concern that getting her mother involved will only make things worse for her. Is it important that school personnel

involve Janice? Consider the legal ramifications if Janice is not informed about the bullying.
6. A number of students have committed suicide following bullying on social media. Does this make it imperative that school personnel get involved or is this problem better solved by parents?
7. Consider personality factors in Hayleigh that make it difficult for her to stand up for herself. Also, consider the frustration of her family members and the program director as they watch Hayleigh lose confidence and become depressed.

Finally, for each of these questions, consider how your own experiences with bullying may impact how you react to the scenario and the approach you may take to address bullying.

REFERENCES

Bauman, S., & Del Rio, A. (2006). Pre-service teachers' response to bullying scenarios: Comparing physical, verbal, and relational bullying. *Journal of Educational Psychology, 98*, 219-231.

Boutlon, M. J. (1997). Teachers' views on bullying: Definitions, attitudes, and ability to cope. *British Journal of Educational Psychology, 67*, 223-233.

Cassidy, W., Faucher, C., & Jackson, M. (2013). Cyberbullying among youth: A comprehensive review of current international research and its implications and application to policy and practice. *School Psychology International: Special Issue on Cyberbullying, 34*(6), 575–612.

Craig, W. M., Currie, C., Grinvoald, H., Dostaler, S., Harel, Y., Hetland, J., ...Pickett, W. (2009). A cross-national profile of bullying typology among young people in 40 countries. *International Journal of Public Health, 5, 216-224.*

Due, P., Holstein, B. E., Lynch, J., Diderichsen, F., Gabhain, S. N., Scheidt, P., Currie, C., & The Health Behaviour in School-Aged Children Bullying Work Group. (2005) Bullying and symptoms among school-aged children: International comparative cross sectional study in 28 countries. *The European Journal of Public Health, 15*, 128–132.

Elgar, F., Craig, W., Boyce, W., Morgan, A., & Vella-Zarb, R. (2009), Income Inequality and School Bullying: Multilevel Study of Adolescents in 37 Countries. *Journal of Adolescent Health, 45*, 341-345.

Feinberg, T., & Robey, N. (2008). Cyberbullying. *Principal Leadership, 9*, 10-14.

Hinduja, S., & Patchin, J. W. (2009). *Bullying beyond the schoolyard: Preventing and responding to cyberbullying.* Thousand Oaks, CA: Sage Publications.

Nansel, T. J., Overpeck, M., Pilla, R. S., Ruan, W. J., Simons-Morton, B., & Scheidt, P. (2001). Bullying behaviors among US youth: Prevalence and associate with psychological adjustment. *Journal of the American Medical Association, 285*, 2094-2100.

Olweus, D. (1993). *Bullying at school: What we know and what we can do.* Oxford: Blackwell.

Olweus, D., & Limber, S. P. (2010). Bullying in School: Evaluation and dissemination of the Olweus Bullying Prevention Program. *American Journal of Orthopsychiatry, 80*, 124-134.

Perkins, H. W., Perkins, J. M., & Craig, D. W. (2009). Where does bullying take place among adolescents when they are at school? Retrieved fromhttp://www.youthhealthsafety.org/bullying.htm

Smith, P. K. (2011). Why interventions to reduce bullying and violence in schools may (or may not) succeed: Comments on this special section. *International Journal of Behavioral Development, 35*, 419-423.

Sullivan, T. N., Farrell, A. D., & Kliewer, W. (2006). Peer victimization in early adolescence: Association between physical and relational victimization and drug use, aggression, and delinquent behaviors among urban middle-school students. *Development and Psychopathology, 18*, 119-137.

Ttofi, M. M., & Farrington, D. P. (2011). Effectiveness of school-based programs to reduce bullying: A systematic and meta-analytic review. *Journal of Experimental Criminology, 7*, 27-56.

Turner, H. A., Finkelhor, D., Hamby, S. L., & Shattuck, A. (2011). Specifying type and location of peer victimization in a national sample of children and youth. *Journal of Youth and Adolescence, 40*, 1052-1067.

Underwood, M. K. (2003). *Social aggression among girls.* New York: Guilford.

III

Issues That Affect the School's Relationship with Stakeholders

Chapter Eight

Autism Spectrum Disorder

Sophie's Journey

Karen L. Dunlap

When parents initially send their child to school, they grant partial control of their most prized possession to persons they may not know and place him/her in a classroom filled with unfamiliar faces, routines, and promises. Hopefully, the learning environment will be one of inspiration and engagement; a place where risk taking is encouraged and diversity valued. Parents of children with special needs have an even greater yearning for assurances that public school classrooms will embrace their child and his/her unique traits.

In this case study, circumstances faced by parents of a toddler diagnosed with autism spectrum disorder (ASD) as they strive to find (a) available educational services and (b) the most appropriate instructional setting for their daughter will be described.

THE CASE STUDY

In the Beginning...

Sophie was a beautiful child. All who saw her were struck by her angelic face accentuated by large deep blue eyes; her long tousled blonde hair tied up in a larger-than-life bow to match her outfit. This was, as her parents loved to tell, the easiest way to keep an eye on her. No one ever had trouble spotting the bow from a distance! Sophie loved the outdoors. Any unhappiness could always be soothed by a walk in the wind; she loved the feel of air as it gently lifted her wispy golden hair and directed it out of her big baby blues. Sophie appeared in every way to be a "normal" two year old girl...until two months into her second year of life, when the following behaviors emerged:

- Loss/avoidance of eye contact with others
- Social skill regression (stopped talking about common occurrences, ceased interacting with both peers and adults, curtailed descriptions of day's activities, etc.).
- Functional speech replaced by "scripted speech" (repeated phrases from books and movies in no particular context)
- Interests restricted
- Creative play subsided

Each of the above behaviors became more pronounced over time. Behavior differences were also noted by the instructors in Sophie's Mother's Day Out program. Sophie was beginning to exhibit noncompliant behaviors and the teachers reported she "could not stay on task," that she would "go off in her own world" seemingly unresponsive to others or her surroundings, and become very upset when changes in routine occurred.

Child Find/Early Intervention

Sophie's parents were acutely aware that something was not right. Both worked in a branch of the medical field and understood full well that something was amiss. Each wanted their daughter to be successful in all aspects of life. To help insure that dream's reality, Sophie's parents sought the advice of her pediatrician who stressed communication and social interaction would be key; therefore, they vowed to find the necessary help for their daughter. Their first question was, where do we go from here?

Through conversations with friends and family, Sophie's parents discovered that the federally mandated Individuals with Disabilities Education Act (IDEA) required each state to have a Child Find/Early Intervention program that targeted early identification of young children within the school district who might benefit from early intervention and special education services. Child Find is a federal mandate under IDEA that requires all school districts to identify, locate, and evaluate all children with disabilities regardless of the severity. As the law states, *The obligation to identify all children who may need special education services exists even if the school is not providing special education services to the child* (Wright & Wright, 2007). In addition, IDEA mandated that each state develop and implement a comprehensive, coordinated system of early intervention services for infants and toddlers with disabilities.

The Early Childhood Intervention (ECI) program was passed by the Texas 67th Legislature in 1961. The program is operated under the Department of

Health and its mission is to identify and provide needed intervention services to children who either have or are at risk of having developmental delays. Eligible children served by the program are from 0-3 years of age and cannot be placed in other programs. ECI attempts to serve qualified children until they are eligible for a district's special education services. Sophie's parents immediately begin to investigate how such a program might help Sophie reach her potential.

The parents were encouraged as the federally mandated ECI program specifically targets children up to three years of age who may benefit from special education services. By utilizing ECI evaluations, a determination as to eligibility and need for services could be assessed at no cost to the family. Once that occurred, the family and school district could work together and plan a program to meet Sophie's unique needs. Therefore, Sophie's parents contacted the school district to schedule the necessary qualifying/testing procedures which needed to be completed prior to Sophie turning three years of age. Time was of the essence. When her parents contacted the school district, they were told there was no room in the testing schedule until sometime *after* Sophie's third birthday.

On Their Own

Sophie's parents, seeing a continual regression in both social and communication skills, decided to look outside the district for additional resources as they awaited a testing date from the district's ECI team. They had Sophie assessed in the private sector by doctors, occupational therapists, and speech diagnosticians. The resulting data showed Sophie had "severely impaired speech" and "severe sensory impairments"; immediately qualifying her for private speech and occupational therapy (OT) services. Without a second thought, Sophie's parents initiated and paid for private speech, OT, and floor-time play-based therapy sessions for their daughter, now age two years, eight months.

From the private therapists, Sophie's parents learned valuable strategies for working with Sophie at home. Techniques to help Sophie learn to use spoken words in context rather than random recitation were initiated by the therapists and followed through by the parents at home. As Sophie's parents better understood the process, they utilized the strategies at home and slowly began to see their daughter attempt a hint of deliberate spoken interaction. Based on these private evaluations, it was determined that Sophie qualified for both cognitive and speech services.

Once the determination was made that Sophie did qualify for ECI for services based upon the findings of the private therapists, Sophie's parents contacted the local school district to begin the assessment/evaluation process at the school district level. Little did Sophie's parents realize the powerful impact that one call would have on plans for Sophie's educational success.

Sophie's parents were hopeful that she would qualify for services through the district and they might be relieved of at least a portion of a very heavy financial obligation. Both parents, however, were determined to work extra jobs, extra hours, whatever it took…to ensure Sophie had all the necessary resources to deal effectively with her ASD. The school district ECI team was not pleased with the private therapists', nor the parent's subsequent follow-ups with district special education personnel, as this triggered a variety of mandated timelines; one of which was that Sophie's Full Individual Evaluation (FIE) had to be completed before her third birthday, which was now less than seven weeks away.

One of the first assessments attempted with Sophie was conducted by the school district's *autism specialist*. Mom and Sophie entered the school building. The specialist was sitting on the floor in a large room when Sophie arrived. As it was late afternoon, buses were noisily pulling up to the school in preparation for after school student boarding. The strange sights and sounds caused Sophie to cling to her mother. The autism specialist attempted to engage Sophie in conversation and activities while remaining on the floor, but to no avail. Sophie and her mother left after just fifteen minutes had passed with no interaction between Sophie and the specialist.

In an effort to solidify Sophie's FIE, a second group of assessments was attempted three weeks prior to Sophie's third birthday. This was known as the Transdisciplinary Play-Based Assessment. The professional team that administered this assessment, based on the Toni Linder Model for assessment, consisted of two Licensed Specialists in School Psychology (LSSP), two speech therapists, an occupational therapist (OT) and a Preschool Program for Children with Disabilities (PPCD) teacher. The parents completed the following rating scales: Behavior Assessment System for Children, 2nd ed., Gilliam Autism Rating Scale, 2nd ed., and the Adaptive Behavior Assessment System, 2nd ed.

Three of the adults from the professional team, including a speech therapist, an OT, and an LSSP diagnostician were on the floor asking Sophie questions and evaluating her responses and/or lack thereof. The evaluators also attempted to get Sophie to engage in play therapy as Sophie's mother sat at a table in the same room with an educational intern. As Sophie was being evaluated, the OT would saunter between the two groups of adults and engage each in conversation. Statements such as, "Where did Sophie get that cute bow?" and "Isn't Sophie just the cutest?" were heard. The entire evaluation session lasted less than forty-five minutes. At its conclusion, the specialists announced Sophie's FIE was complete and they would be in touch with the parents as to the results.

One week later, prior to the scheduling of an Admission, Review, and Dismissal (ARD) meeting, the school district contacted Sophie's parents to go over the final FIE results. Apprehension filled the air as they walked into the school's conference room. What would the report reveal about the challenges their daughter was facing? More importantly, what services were available to help her? Finally, all personnel from the transdisciplinary assessment team and Sophie's parents were at the table...and...Sophie's parents were told...she did *not* qualify for *any* services! *What?* Instead, many compliments about how cute Sophie was dominated the conversation from most members of the FIE evaluation team members.

One participating team member suggested Sophie be given a pair of scissors to enhance her fine-motor skills prior to kindergarten enrollment. Sophie's parents left the meeting bewildered and confused. With the formal district ARD meeting set to convene soon, Sophie's parents studied their options. It should come as no surprise that at the ensuing ARD meeting, both parents disagreed with the denial of district services and insisted Sophie be observed by appropriate school district personnel in a peer setting so interaction and communication might be authentically assessed.

Observation among Peers

During the FIE assessment and evaluation period, Sophie had continued her enrollment in the local Mother's Day Out (MDO) program. This was deemed the perfect setting for school district personnel to observe Sophie's social and communicative tendencies as it (a) was a familiar and comfortable setting for Sophie, and (b) would provide interactional peer data that previous observations had not captured. Upon parental request, a Board Certified Behavior Analyst (BCBA) was reluctantly sent by the district to observe Sophie.

The BCBA went right to the MDO classroom where the teachers were a bit confused as they had not been informed an observation was to take place that day. The MDO instructors called Sophie's parents a bit irritated that they were not made aware of the impending assessment. Sophie's mother apologized to all MDO staff and explained she had no idea the BCBA would show up that day as she had not been informed of the visit either. After consultation, MDO teachers consented to the observation, but informed the BCBA that it was currently naptime and Sophie was sleeping. The BCBA left immediately after Sophie awoke from her nap.

Upon receipt of the naptime evaluation notes, Sophie's parents were livid. Not only was the assessment, in their opinion, bogus; the evaluator appeared to have gone to the school without knowledge or consent of either them or MDO staff/personnel.

One of Sophie's private therapists, trained in Applied Behavior Analysis (ABA), suggested that before convening the next ARD, it might be a good idea to request a special education teacher familiar with ABA also observe their daughter at MDO. This would provide additional data that would help the ARD committee make an informed decision regarding Sophie's future educational placement and services. Both parents agreed and that observation was arranged with school district approval.

Preschool Program for Children with Disabilities (PPCD Placement)

Based on the district's special education assessment and an ARD, where qualification for special education services were discussed and granted, Sophie was placed in the district's PPCD class for the remaining three months of the school year. Sophie's first day in PPCD was actually the day after her third birthday. No OT or speech services were offered by the district, so private sector services were maintained by the family.

It took Sophie several weeks to adjust to her new surroundings. New faces, new smells, new sounds, new routines, and a new teacher all played a part in disrupting her communication/social progress. The PPCD teacher, however, was acutely aware of Sophie and her unique needs. As Sophie grew accustomed to the new environment, her teacher saw within her unleashed potential. The PPCD teacher noticed Sophie's mind functioned as a sponge...she soaked up content beyond the capabilities of other students in the PPCD class.

While words in context were not consistently utilized, the PPCD teacher believed this would happen quicker if Sophie spent time with nondisabled peers and heard their conversations. Therefore, the PPCD teacher established a unique schedule for Sophie; one that would help her progress. During part of the day, Sophie stayed in the PPCD classroom interacting with students her age; during another time slot, she spent working with students in *the regular* preschool classroom. In this setting, Sophie excelled.

As summer approached, her parents requested extended school year (ESY) in an effort to minimize any potential skill regression. Their request was denied by the school district despite a doctor's written official diagnosis of ASD and recommendation for the placement. Therefore, over the summer, Sophie's parents relied once again on the private sector as Sophie continued to see her OT, speech therapist, and newly hired ABA specialist. Her parents were determined to garner all available resources to minimize any potential regression in skills previously attained.

Private School

As summer drew to a close, the ARD meeting to set up Sophie's preschool placement was scheduled. The doctor who diagnosed Sophie's ASD during his evaluation suggested Sophie had improved socially to the point she would benefit from interaction with neurotypical peers; that is, children of similar age and development without any developmental disabilities. That recommendation was taken to the ARD committee as both her doctors and parents felt it reflected the least restrictive environment for Sophie.

Initial talks found the district offering mainstream preschool. However, within this setting, no special education curriculum would be offered and no outside therapists would be permitted to work with the preschool teacher. It was suggested that Sophie's parents consider utilizing a daycare or Head Start program. Therefore, Sophie's parents denied the placement. The two sides continued to talk and the district finally compromised by permitting Sophie to attend weekly speech therapy sessions at the elementary school as a transition activity. For this her parents were grateful.

Frustrated, Sophie's parents looked yet again to the private sector, this time at private preschools available in the area. After numerous interviews, they decided on a private school placement for Sophie. This school's administration permitted inclusion of outside the classroom ABA, speech, and OT therapists. The educational team felt all children would benefit from the visual curriculum and other ABA strategies provided for Sophie.

Next Steps?

Sophie's placement in the private preschool setting was a beneficial one. While there were some challenges, there were also many successes. Due to the intense early intervention strategies, therapies, and programs, Sophie exhibited dramatic improvement. She discovered language. Sophie discovered words have power. Less than one year after engaging in multiple early intervention strategies and therapies, Sophie met or exceeded all developmental milestones for her age and

- eye contact returned;
- keen interest in socialization emerged and appropriate peer interactions occurred daily;
- functional language was utilized and most scripted speech was eliminated;
- and creative and pretend play occurred.

Throughout this entire time period, Sophie's parents continued all private therapies while working with the school district in preparation for Sophie's transition to public school kindergarten.

The superintendent in the district found an affinity for Sophie and her parents after some personal conversations he had with them about their daughter throughout the ordeal with the special education educators. He volunteered to observe Sophie on his own time. He also requested that he receive periodic documentation of her educational progress. Once that process was in place, the school district superintendent began to work in conjunction with the district ARD committee. Through this and other collaborative efforts of the superintendent, the district compromised and offered to allow all current therapies to be continued during Sophie's formal transition period into general education kindergarten when she turned five years of age.

All educational stakeholders including parents, a developmental pediatrician, district personnel, and therapists agreed that the best plan for Sophie was to wean her off all therapies gradually when she showed readiness and ability to function successfully without them. Through a long process that is still evolving, the development of an initial sense of respect and feeling of trust resulting from collaboration between all stakeholders finally succeeded where individual agendas had not. The dream that Sophie one day might be indistinguishable from her nondisabled peers despite her ASD now appears to be a bit closer to reality.

THE LITERATURE REVIEW

The information utilized in this case study is derived from a compilation of both current and foundational literature topics that address the use of early intervention techniques with children on the ASD spectrum. This literature review focuses on the following topics:

- Prevalence of ASD Diagnosis: Girls vs. Boys
- Early Intervention
- Educational Service Providers
- Financial Constraints

Prevalence of ASD Diagnosis: Girls vs. Boys

According to the Center for Disease Control and Prevention (2015), autism affects one in sixty-eight children and approximately five times as many boys as girls, thus raising a distinct possibility that girls who are on the spectrum may go undetected (Baio, 2014; Dworzynski et al., 2012). Some studies suggested this occurs due to the fact that a girl's failure to make eye contact may be initially mistaken for shyness, apprehension, nervousness, being bashful or quiet, etc., rather than as a sign of autism spectrum disorder or ASD (Lee, 2012; Wright, 2011).

Additional theories contended girls may appear on the autistic spectrum less often as they are often not as aggressive or disruptive in their actions because they try to mimic behaviors in order to be socially accepted by their peers (Sarris, 2013; Wagner, 2006). It should also be noted ASD research shows the condition does not favor any particular racial, ethnic and/or socioeconomic group (Klaiman et al., 2015).

Early Intervention

Subtle signs of developmental disorders are often present in early infancy. Indeed, parents of young children are frequently the first to notice that something is awry in their child's social or emotional behavior; especially if a failure to develop functional language is noted. According to The New England Center for Children (2015), the following characteristics are critical to an ASD diagnosis:

1. Impairment in social interaction (e.g., limited eye contact, responding to people as if they are objects).
2. Communicative deficits (e.g., limited or no verbal communicative skills, problems using pronouns).
3. Repetitive behavior or marked adherence to specific routines (e.g., problems transitioning from one activity or environment to another). (para. 2)

Research findings have suggested that ASD children who receive early intensive, individualized behavioral interventions often make such significant progress they are able to drop the diagnosis of autism (Holm, 2014). One such early intervention process is Applied Behavior Analysis (ABA) which analyzes each child's unique skill deficits/problem behaviors and seeks resolution through direct instruction. Therefore, specific instruction can be tailored to particular situational needs (Wagner, Wallace, & Rogers, 2014).

An additional intervention is federally mandated by the Individuals with Disabilities Education Act (IDEA). Part C of this act affords parents the opportunity to procure services for their birth to three-year-old child if certain criteria are met. Early Intervention (EI) services are designed to help younger children who possess uncharacteristic physical cognitive, adaptive, communication and/or social/emotional development (Nahmias, Kase, & Mandell, 2014). IDEA mandates qualified children receive necessary services in an accepted setting conducted by trained/qualified personnel.

Parents of toddlers who meet state criteria must be informed of "availability of services under section 619 of IDEA, Part C, not fewer than 90 days prior to the toddler's third birthday" (Center for Parent Information and Resources, 2014, Handout 5 §303.301(3)c). Once children reach age three, they transition to services provided under Part B of IDEA. Services are generally available to parents at no cost. A child's parents or his/her physician may initiate the referral process described in IDEA's Child Find mandate.

Each state, therefore, is charged with the development of a comprehensive system of early intervention services for infants and toddlers with disabilities. This Early Childhood Intervention (ECI) program requires all school districts to identify and evaluate young children suspected of having a disability in an effort to alleviate deficits that could potentially disrupt their ability to function effectively socially, emotionally, or academically with his/her peer group (Brian, Bryson, & Zwaigenbaum, 2015). It should be noted that once parents consent to an ECI evaluation of their son/daughter, the assessment and ensuing results *must* be completed and reported within a state-specified time frame (Macy, Marks, & Towle, 2014).

Educational Service Providers

A dilemma becoming more and more common is that of parental school choice when identifying the best instructional setting for their child. No longer is the neighborhood school always perceived as the "best" choice (Boswell, Zablotsky, & Smith, 2014). Availability and differentiation of services offered by public and/or private educational institutions can become jungles to negotiate.

Parents of children with ASD and other social difficulties often struggle with the home-school relationship as they strive to build trusting relationships (Stoner et al., 2005). At times, even though school personnel state they understand the challenges parents of ASD children face, parents frequently become skeptical when a decision is made by district personnel that is perceived as unfounded or detrimental to the best interest of the child (Iadarola et al., 2014).

Tension between the two sides may also be exacerbated by other factors, such as alleged issues of power, knowledge and life experiences (Bitterman et al., 2008). Therefore, home-school relations can be fragile if not built on foundations of trust and approachability (Broomhead, 2013).

Once a child is tested and results disseminated to the parents, the decision to accept the findings rests with the parents. If they disagree with services offered by a public school, the options shift to include investigation of services rendered by private schools and/or other private entities. It should be noted that a special education student attending a private institution does not have the same legal rights to services as one in public school; as IDEA mandates only pertain to public institutions unless the school district cannot provide an appropriate placement (Special Education Law: The Individuals with Disabilities Education Act, 2009).

Financial Constraints

According to the most recent Center for Disease Control estimates (2014), the cost of caring for a child with autism spectrum disorder (ASD) is approximately $17,000 more per year compared to a child without the disorder. Costs include, but are not limited to health care, education, ASD-related therapy, family services, and caregiver time (Lavelle et al., 2014).

Applied Behavior Analysis (ABA) can also be expensive; many times costing in upwards of $30,000 per year (University of Missouri-Columbia, 2008). Families of children with ASD, therefore, bare heavy out-of-pocket costs. Additionally, parents must face the challenge of health care insurance coverages and reimbursements as at the present time there is no guarantee that procedures covered today will be included in policies of the future (Parish et al., 2015).

Further, parents may decide that private education schools are the better option as such facilities often have smaller class sizes where teachers are able to monitor student progress and care for unique needs in a more personalized environment than their public school counterparts (Harrell, 2009). However, it should be noted that along with the customization comes the high cost of private school tuition.

The Guiding Questions

The following questions are presented to encourage critical analysis of the case study. Formulate your answers by using knowledge of district policies (both public and private), the requirements of IDEA referred to in this case scenario, as well as the Child Find and ECI components of the federally mandated program.

1. As the number of children with diagnosed ASD at an early age increases, an even greater demand for early intervention services will be placed on both public and private institutions. How might public schools do a better job of helping parents navigate the often convoluted path of assessment, evaluation, qualification, and placement? How might private school personnel acquire additional knowledge and expertise/change policies and/or procedures to help identify children who may be on the spectrum and insure appropriate placement for parents who choose this avenue? How might public and private schools create partnerships to help stem the high cost of appropriate services for both the institution and the parent(s)?
2. Early intervention teams are charged with identifying children who qualify for ASD and recommending appropriate educational services. Under what circumstances should public school specialists be permit-

ted to work with an ASD child attending private school and vice versa? What might be some implications from such practices? What can be done to foster collaboration/seamless sharing of information between diagnosticians, occupational therapists, ABA therapists, etc., of a child whose parents may be using a mix of specialists from both the public school and private sectors (both during the early identification phase and beyond)?
3. What are some strategies ARD committee personnel might use to help ease parental anxiety and/or diffuse angry emotions when negotiations concerning their child's placement are ongoing?

FINAL CONSIDERATIONS

Some final considerations for assistance in contemplating possible solutions to the problems above are offered. Remember, the questions above have no static right or wrong answers. The right solution is the one that follows the intent of the law (in this case IDEA and its connections to both Child Find and ECI programs) and is based on appropriate supporting evidence/documentation that reflects an appropriate placement for a child on the autism spectrum.

To successfully navigate the process of procuring the best educational placement for a child with special needs, parents and educators need to collaborate in an effort to create a learning environment that best addresses the child's unique needs (Turnbull et al., 2015).

All educators on the child's team must be able to formulate rationales for their decisions in language that is both appropriate and understandable to all stakeholders, including parents/guardians. Instead of simply pushing papers, educators would do well to get the parent's thoughts as well...to treat them as partners, not merely patrons. Parents should not be afraid to explain the uniqueness of their child, to brainstorm ideas, to entertain new and different ways to meet specific objectives or timelines, or to speak their concerns in honest dialogue, even if it means disagreeing with the educational diagnostic team and their initial results. Collaboration by trust outplays egos and personal agendas.

Adults on both sides should not be afraid to take a second look at the situation if anything about it doesn't seem quite right. Moving too quickly and simply closing the door on the offering of any potential services may not be the best solution for the school district, the educator or the child. If potential traits of ASD go undetected for years, an undiagnosed child loses valuable time that could be spent working with therapists and learning to overcome some characteristics of the condition that might plague them unnecessarily at a later date (Moore, 2016).

Indeed, ideas, strategies and plans that are deemed appropriate for students on the autistic spectrum may also benefit their neurotypical peers. Early identification of possible features of ASD in toddlers and the accompanying appropriate therapy in addition to the building of a collaborative relationship among all stakeholders will help ensure the educational journey is a rewarding one.

REFERENCES

Baio, J. (2014). Prevalence of autism spectrum disorder among children aged 8 years—Autism and developmental disabilities monitoring network, 11 sites, United States, 2010. Morbidity and Mortality Weekly Report (MMWR), 63 (SS02); 1-21. Retrieved from: http://www.cdc.gov/mmwr/preview/mmwrhtml/ss6302a1.htm?s_cid=ss6302a1_w

Bitterman, A., Daley, T., Misra, S., Carlson, E., & Markowitz, J. (2008). A national sample of preschoolers with autism spectrum disorders: Special education services and parent satisfaction. *Journal of Autism and Developmental Disorders, 38*(8), 1509-1517.

Boswell, K., Zablotsky, B., & Smith, C. (2014). Predictors of Autism enrollment in Public School Systems. *Exceptional Children, 80*(1), 96-106. Doi: 10.1177/0014402914532230

Brian, J., Bryson, S., & Zwaigenbaum, L. (2015). Autism spectrum disorder in infancy: developmental considerations in treatment targets. *Current Opinion in Neurology, 28(2)*, 117-123.

Broomhead, K. (2013). Blame, guilt and the need for "labels": Insights from parents of children with special educational needs and educational practitioners. *British Journal of Special Education, 40*(1), 14-21. Doi: 10.1111/1467-8578.12012

Center for Parent Information and Resources. (2014, September). *Public awareness and the central directory (IDEA's verbatim regulations)*. Retrieved from www.parentcenterhub.org/repository/partc-module3.

Centers for Disease Control and Prevention. (2015, February 26). *Data & statistics*. Retrieved from: http://www.cdc.gov/ncbddd/autism/data.html

Dworzynski, K., Ronald, A., Bolton, P., & Happé, F. (2012). How different are girls and boys above and below the diagnostic threshold for autism spectrum disorders? *Journal of the American Academy of Child & Adolescent Psychiatry, 51*(8), 788-97 doi: 10.1016/j.jaac.2012.05.018

Harrell, C. (2009). Special needs education—Public or private school? *Ezine*. Retrieved from http://ezinearticles.com/?Special-Needs-Education---Public-Or-Private-School?&id=3435619

Holm, A. (2014). *Outcome in adulthood for children with autism spectrum disorder who have received early intensive behavioral intervention*. (Master's Thesis). Available from HF-Master Theses. Retrieved from http://hdl.handle.net/10642/2173

Iadarola, S., Hetherington, S., Clinton, C., Dean, M., Reisinger, E., Huynh, L., Locke, J., Conn, K., Heinert, S., Kataoka, S., Harwood, R., Smith, T., Mandell, D., & Kasari, C. (2014, September 5). Services for children with autism spectrum disorder in three, large urban school districts: Perspectives of parents and educators. Autism. Advanced online publication. Doi: 1362361314548078

Klaiman, C., Fernandez-Carriba, S., Hall, C., & Saulnier, C. (2015). Assessment of autism across the lifespan: A way forward. *Current Developmental Disorders Reports*, 2(1), 84-92. Doi: 10.1007/s40474-014-0031-5

Lavelle, T., Weinstein, M., Newhouse, J., Munir, K., Kuhlthau, K., & Prosser, L. (2014). Economic burden of childhood autism spectrum disorders. *Pediatrics, 133*(3). Doi: 10.1542/peds.2013-0763.

Lee, J. (2012, September 3). *Diagnosis eludes many girls with autism, study says*. Simons Foundation Autism Research Initiative. Retrieved from: http://sfari.org/news-and-opinion/news/2012/diagnosis-eludes-many-girls-with-autism-study-says

Macy, M., Marks, K., & Towle, A. (2014). Missed, misused, or mismanaged: Improving early detection systems to optimize child outcomes. *Topics in Early Childhood Special Education, 24*(2), 94-105.

Moore, D. (2016). The fourth degree of autism: The self-identification. In P. Wylie, W. Lawson, & L. Beardon (Eds.), *The nine degrees of autism: A developmental model* (pp. 85-108). New York, NY: Routledge

Nahmias, A., Kase, C., & Mandell, D. (2014). Comparing cognitive outcomes among children with autism spectrum disorders receiving community-based early intervention in one of three placements. *Autism, 18*(3), 311-320.

Parish, S., Thomas, K., Williams, C., & Crossman, M. (2015). Autism and families' financial burden. *The Association with Health Insurance Coverage American Journal on Intellectual and Developmental Disabilities, 120*(2), 166-175. Doi: 10.1352/1944-7558-120.2.166

Sarris, M. (2013, February 19). Not just for boys: When autism spectrum disorders affect girls. Retrieved from: http://iancommunity.org/cs/simons_simplex_community/autism_in_girls

Special education law: The Individuals with Disabilities Education Act. (2009). Retrieved from http://www.understandingspecialeducation.com/special-education-law.html

Stoner, J., Bock, S., Thompson, J., Angeli, M., Heyl, B., & Crowley, P. (2005). Welcome to our world: Parent perceptions of interactions between parents of young children with ASD and education professionals. *Focus on Autism and Other Developmental Disabilities, 20*(1). 39-51. Doi: 10.1177/10883576050200001040 1

The New England Center for Children. (2015). *What is autism?* Retrieved from: http://www.necc.org/research/understanding-autism.aspx

Turnbull, A., Turnbull, H., Erwin, E., Soodak, L., & Shogren, K. (2015). *Families, professionals, and exceptionality: Positive outcomes through partnerships and trust.* Pearson.

Wagner, A., Wallace, K., & Rogers, S. (2014). Developmental approaches to treatment of young children with autism spectrum disorder. In J. Tarbox, D. Dixon, P. Sturmey, & J. Matson (Eds.), *Handbook of Early Intervention for Autism Spectrum Disorders: Research, Policy, and Practice* (393-428). New York: Springer.

Wagner, S. (2006). Educating the female student with Asperger's. In *Asperger's and Girls*. Arlington, TX: Future Horizons Inc.

Wright, J. (2011, January 13). Gender bias. [Blog post]. Retrieved from: http://sfari.org/news-and-opinion/blog/2011/gender-bias

Wright, P., & Wright, P. (2007). *Wrightslaw: Special education law* (2nd Edition). Hartfield, VA: Harbor House Law Press, Inc.

University of Missouri-Columbia. (2008, February 29). Financial struggles plague families of children with autism. *ScienceDaily*. Retrieved June 15, 2015 from www.sciencedaily.com/releases/2008/02/080229105843.htm

Chapter Nine

Every Student Counts

Did She Really Say That?

Teresa Starrett

Assessment and achievement are prevalent themes on every campus throughout the country. Educators are under scrutiny to ensure all students meet expectations regardless of background, ability or resources available. However, there are often circumstances that come into play that are not clear at first glance, as the following case study showcases:

CASE STUDY

Smithville Elementary, located in the outskirts of a large urban district serves a diverse student population. Of the 750 K-5 students who attend the school, 52% are Hispanic, 29% White, 13% African American, 4% Asian, and 2% identify as two or more races. While 61% of the students are eligible for free or reduced lunch, 18% are Limited English Proficient and 49% are considered at-risk.

Despite these challenges, Smithville Elementary has an active and involved parent base, a high quality teaching staff, and students who continue to achieve academically. Due to the high achievement and best practices at Smithville, the school was recognized nationally as a Blue Ribbon School.

As Mrs. Stilwell, principal at Smithville Elementary, walked the halls of the school this Wednesday morning, it was uncharacteristically quiet. During her daily walkthroughs, the classroom doors were shut, students' heads were bent in concentration, and teachers were walking up and down the rows of desks. This was in sharp contrast to what Mrs. Stilwell normally saw: doors open, learning noise and student movement within each class. Generally, this would be alarming; however, today was state testing day, and everything was running like clockwork.

She greeted the hall monitors who allowed students to go to the restroom one by one, and headed back to the office secure in the knowledge that all was well. Yes, teachers are compliant with testing procedures, Mrs. Stilwell mused, but are we doing what is best for students? She reflected on a brief discussion with Mr. Jensen, the assistant principal that morning. Though she had not had an opportunity to discuss his concerns in depth, he indicated he needed to talk with her about a staff member. Those discussions never end well, Mrs. Stilwell thought.

The motto of Smithville—"To teach and inspire; to reach and transform. Every student. Every year"—was evident in the actions of most parents, teachers, and students. Mrs. Stilwell and her administrative team, with the help of selected teachers, thoughtfully hired new faculty and provided support for them through their induction year, conducted continual data analysis to assess student needs, and evaluate the effectiveness of programs. However, there were some issues that continued to bother her. Should she expect perfection?

She knew there were some individuals who believed her expectations were unrealistic as she truly expected each child at Smithville to thrive and achieve. In order to best meet the needs of all students, two years ago the campus conducted a needs assessment to determine the teachers' level of understanding regarding Response to Intervention (RTI). Surprisingly, the results were mixed. It was found that, while many teachers had heard of RTI, their definitions of the process and how these interventions could assist students were vastly different.

Determined to combat this, Mrs. Stilwell worked to provide clear and ongoing professional development that would first define RTI, provide a structure for the campus, assess students to determine needs, and provide assistance for those at the highest level of intervention. Mr. Jensen, assistant principal, pokes his head into Mrs. Stilwell's office and says, "Do you have a moment?" He, then, shut the door and took a seat. Mrs. Stilwell raised her eyebrow and asked, "Okay, spill it. What happened?"

Mr. Jensen explained during a Student Support Team (SST) meeting, where teachers bring concerns about students who have behaviors or academics that require additional intervention according to the proposed RTI model, there was an interaction that left him concerned. The parent, general education teacher, intervention specialist, and counselor were all present. The student, a third grader, was experiencing some difficulty with behavior. Specifically, his teacher reported noncompliance with rules, talking in class, and some out of seat behavior.

However, none of these behaviors had resulted in an office referral. The teacher indicated different strategies, including a token system, were attempted. In addition to the behavior concerns, scores on curriculum-based assessments in reading were at the second grade level with scattered skills from 2.0-2.6. The teacher was accommodating in the classroom, but the content was becoming more difficult; therefore, an additional level of assistance was requested.

According to Mr. Jensen, the teacher and the parent had communicated about these difficulties and, though the parent was concerned, she agreed to the additional intervention. Mr. Jensen indicated the parent was visibly nervous at this time and began wringing her hands. She asked if perhaps a change of teacher might be beneficial—if a different teaching style might be what the child needs rather than extra help. At this time, the counselor, Mrs. Porter, replied, "You know, maybe public school is not the right place for him."

Mr. Jensen indicated he jumped in and said, "We are certainly well qualified to educate James. I think this plan to provide extra support with academics will be extremely helpful for him." He closed the meeting shortly after that. Mrs. Stilwell raised her eyebrow at Mr. Jensen again and thanked him for the information and let him know she needed to have a bit of time to think.

At the end of the day, all teachers returned their materials to the office where Mr. Jensen compared the serial numbers, accounted for all test booklets, and readied them for shipment. After the last test had been accounted for, Mrs. Stilwell and Mr. Jensen marveled at the smooth day and attributed it to the professional development provided at the monthly faculty meeting.

"It was like a well-oiled machine," thought Mrs. Stilwell, *except* for James's test. His teacher said he had repeatedly gone to the bathroom, complained of a stomachache, and finally put his head down refusing to continue. When asked why she didn't contact the office, the teacher said, "That is just James. It is what he does."

Thursday morning, as she was about to conduct her rounds, the secretary let Mrs. Stilwell know the district area superintendent was on the phone indicating it was urgent. Mrs. Stilwell took the call and was asked if she had run the absence numbers for the test the previous day. Knowing this was an important part of testing and accountability, she answered in the affirmative. Still puzzled, she asked why this was relevant. Dr. Santos, the area superintendent, shared she had received a phone call from four parents voicing concerns.

These four parents had students who received differentiated instruction under the RTI model, based upon skills assessed. The parents reported they had been advised that the state test was not appropriate because the latest assessment data indicated they were achieving below grade level and it would be best for them to stay home. Three of the four students did, indeed, do that. Mrs. Stilwell asked Dr. Santos who phoned the parents and she responded, "The parents say a lady who works with their children." Mrs. Stilwell assured her she would investigate and get back to her by the end of the day.

The pieces of the puzzle began falling into place for Mrs. Stilwell then. The SST meeting, James struggling on state testing, and students being asked to stay home. It was 8:30 and she had the day to solve the mystery and to fix what could potentially be an assessment and compliance nightmare.

The first thing Mrs. Stilwell did was pull the assessment data for James and the four students. Based upon whole class achievement screening instruments, these five students were achieving more than one grade level below their peers in reading. In accordance with the RTI structure put in place, the students should have been placed in Tier 1 interventions within the classroom and data should have been collected. Then, more intensive interventions should have occurred. However, as Mrs. Stilwell found, the data trail ended with the initial assessment. Where to begin?

THE LITERATURE REVIEW

Campuses must work to identify the needs of students and how they can best intervene. In an effort to do this, Response to Intervention (RTI) is the required process. RTI incorporates the practice of five essential components into one system. Present in the effective RTI program are (1) high-quality, research-based instruction that meets the needs of every student, (2) achievement or behavior performance screeners, (3) evidence-based interventions, (4) progress monitoring tools to collect data, and (5) the ability to make informed educational decisions with the data collected, data-based decision-making (Mellard, McKnight, & Woods, 2009; Hoover & Love, 2011).

The process of RTI encompasses the concepts of high-quality, scientific-based classroom instruction; multiple assessment tools, including screeners and formative standardized tests; frequent and ongoing progress monitoring; research-based methods of intervention implemented according to the student's individual needs; data-based educational decisions; continuous communication and professional development of all staff responsible for the learning environment (Mellard, McKnight, & Woods, 2009; Hoover & Love, 2011).

The first step in the RTI process is the administration of a reliable, valid, and balance accuracy universal screener that determines or predicts which students are at-risk for failure on future performance evaluations (Mellard, McKnight & Woods, 2009). The goal is to identify a majority of the at-risk students with the use of this screener with the assessment being administered school-wide up to three times a year. Analysis of scores is crucial to the decision-making process and is generally conducted by teams of teachers.

Education professionals use assessments to determine the level of support needed by the individual student and develop a plan for targeted and systematic interventions (McCue, 2010). The intensity level of the interventions is then increased after a period of unresponsive progress monitoring.

Tier 1 interventions include a standards-based core curriculum within general education classrooms. Tier 1 consists of high-quality differentiated instruction with the use of flexible groupings in a whole class setting. The first tier includes 80-85% of students who receive evidence-based instruction incorporating best teaching practices.

Tier 2 interventions are supplemental to instruction and meet specific needs of a student once a gap is identified. Usually provided in a small-group setting, Tier 2 interventions allocate more time for practicing concepts and intensify the instructional strategies being implemented. Tier 2 interventions increase with intensity and frequency and include additional practice or the reteaching of concepts. Approximately 10-15% of struggling learners are identified through the screening process as needing additional support in a small group setting on the second level of RTI.

Tier 3 interventions consist of even more intensive, specialized instruction administered to the student one-on-one (Hoover & Love, 2011). After gathering data from multiple sources including assessments, screeners, teacher input, and progress monitoring charts, educational decisions are made about why the student is not responding to instruction or interventions (Samuels, 2008). Tier 3 interventions are more intensive, more frequent and increase in duration with the possibility of a referral to special education after the analysis of a variety of collected data (Johnson et al., 2006). The final tier includes specially designed instruction taught in a one-on-one environment for a very small group of students.

Successful implementation of the RTI process begins with a shared vision and collaborative leadership. Administrators must stress fidelity, provide resources, structure time for interventions, create teacher "buy-in," and be knowledgeable about all components of the process. Johnson and Smith (2011) emphasize the need for leaders to set high expectations for campus teachers to implement research-based strategies properly.

Fidelity of implementation is necessary to guarantee accurate data is collected (Johnson et al., 2006). Leaders are responsible for providing the essential resources to ensure effective classroom practices. Additionally, a problem-solving team optimally should be responsible for ensuring teachers are aware of strategies utilized with students who are identified at-risk (McCue, 2010).

THE GUIDING QUESTIONS

The following questions are presented to help you think critically about the case study. Answer them by referencing your state educator code, assessment policies and law.

1. Describe the process Mrs. Stilwell must go through to investigate the situation Dr. Santos described. What are the steps she should take once she determines the person who called the families?
2. Research the legality of the statement, "You know, maybe public school is not the right place for him." What are the potential ramifications of this?
3. Role-play the discussion you would have with the school counselor regarding her comments to James's mother. Should this wait until the investigation into regarding the parent phone calls is complete? Who should be involved in this meeting? Would this discussion be different if she was the one who called the other parents?
4. As a part of a monthly conference with each grade level team, you require each teacher to bring his or her class set of data. You find the teachers are interpreting the data sets incorrectly. Describe the process of disaggregating data as though you were having a "data chat" with a teacher. Provide a rationale regarding why this is an essential skill at the classroom level.
5. You are meeting with James's teacher. For this meeting, you have asked her to bring the current assessment data for the students in her class and her interpretation of these scores. When discussing these results, you find she has been interpreting the initial data set and not reassessing students for growth. What additional professional development do you need to provide for teachers in order to best serve the students on your campus?
6. Describe, in detail, the type of data disaggregation a teacher must be able to do in order to adjust instruction. What is the principal's role in ensuring teachers have these skills?
7. Explain the purpose of RTI and how assessment should be used to support student success. Identify the leader's role in assessment and the oversight of RTI.

FINAL CONSIDERATIONS

Some final considerations to the problem above are discussed below. In an effort to best serve students of all abilities and needs, the school leader must establish a clear mission and vision and articulate this. As you work through the questions above, consider the following:

1. When discussing a complaint, gather as much information as possible. Half facts can make an investigation much more difficult.
2. Public versus private—it is necessary to understand the school's responsibility in the education of a child.
3. Prior to meetings such as this, it is important to ensure you are fully prepared. Determine how this conversation with the counselor would be documented.
4. Does your district have a structure in place for teacher data chats? How are these conducted?
5. How is school data presented to teachers? How is this analyzed collectively and in PLCs?
6. Access your campus RTI procedure. How does this compare to a model policy?

REFERENCES

Hoover, J., & Love, E. (2011). Supporting school-based response to intervention: A practitioner's mode. *Teaching Exceptional Children, 43*(3), 40.

Johnson, E., Mellard, D. F., Fuchs, D., & McKnight, M. A. (2006). *Responsiveness to intervention: How to do it.* Lawrence, KS: National Research Center on Learning Disabilities.

Johnson, E. S., & Smith, L. A. (2011). Response to intervention in middle school: A case story. *Middle School Journal, 42*(3), 24-32.

McCue, P. (2010). Closing the loop on classroom interventions. *Principal Leadership, 11*(4), 56-61.

Mellard, D. F., McKnight, M., & Woods, K. (2009). Response to intervention screening and progress-monitoring practices in 41 local schools. *Learning Disabilities Research & Practice, 24*, 186-195.

Samuels, C. A. (2008). Responsive teaching. Education Week Teacher Professional Development Sourcebook. Retrieved from: http://www.edweek.org/tsb/articles/2008/09/10/01rti.h02.html

United States Department of Education (2015). National blue ribbon schools programs. Retrieved from: http://www2.ed.gov/programs/nclbbrs/awards.html

Chapter Ten

Teaching Students to Learn or Teaching to the Test?

Patrick M. Jenlink

The following focuses on ethical issues and problems that can be seen in the hiring and standardized testing practices that unfold throughout the case study. The issues that effervesce due to these issues make for a situation where the students ultimately lose. Both leadership and teaching practices become the focal point in what follows.

THE CASE STUDY

The Educational Setting

The scenario depicted in this case took place during the 2012-2013 academic year at Stromberg Elementary, a K-6 public elementary school in the Maleficent Independent School District. The administrative staff consists of an African American principal, Mrs. Wolverton, who's been the administrator for six years and a first year African American male assistant principal, Mr. Perrault, who was referred to the position by the principal. The administrative staff includes a counselor, Mrs. Fanning, an African American female, who is a relative to the principal, and a nurse, Mrs. Copley, and various office staff; all are either African-American or Latino. All the office staff was recommended for hire by the principal due to their personal ties.

Stromberg Elementary has approximately 650 students from K-6th grades, with approximately five or six teachers at each grade, depending on the grade, and not including two resource teachers and a special education team leader. The demographics of teaching staff consisted of 99.5% African Americans, with three males and 0.5 % female Caucasians. The demographics of the student population consists of 99% African-Americans, 0.5% Hispanics, 0.2 Asians, and 0.3% Caucasians.

The student population is 89% targeted as disadvantaged. The racial profile of the community that the campus serves is comprised of approximately 90% African-American, 6% Caucasian, 2% Hispanic, and 1% defined as either Asian or Pacific Islander. The economy of the community is primarily middle income.

The Scenario

For the past six years, the accountability rating of Stromberg Elementary had steadily increased from acceptable to recognized. The Accountability Rating System for Texas Public Schools and School Districts used a subset of the performance measures computed to assign a rating to each public school and district. Performance on each of these indicators is shown disaggregated by ethnicity, special education, low income status, Limited English Proficient status, at-risk status (district, region, and state), and by bilingual/ESL (district, region, and state) (TEA, 2015a).

In the last year, the campus increased dramatically in science and math, raising an average of 45 points in 5th grade science and approximately 30% for math in grades 3-6, as found in the campus' Academic Excellence Indicator System (AEIS) reports, which is used for reporting a wide range of information on the performance of students in each school and district in Texas every year. This information is put into the annual AEIS reports, which are available each year in the fall (see TEA, 2015b).

The administration team, in order to move the rating from acceptable (met the state requirement regarding performance on state standardized testing, completion rate, annual dropout rate, and the progress of English Language Learners) to recognized (scored beyond acceptable), had implemented strategies for success that targets an increase in subpopulations, such as alternate state standardized test, the Texas Assessment of Knowledge and Skills (TAKS) and English as a second language. No one had really questioned the administration's strategies, or suspected that the strategies were anything but appropriate.

The scenario begins with a teacher, Mrs. Struppe, who had been recommended for hire by Mrs. Wolverton the principal. Mrs. Struppe is an army veteran accustomed to following orders with 5 years' experience teaching in K-5 education. She had previously taught grades 2-3 in a combined classroom for one year before she joined the 4th grade team, in which Mrs. Staunton served as team leader. In speaking with Mrs. Struppe during math planning, Mrs. Staunton reflected on Mrs. Struppe's comment that although she would collaborate with the 4th grade team on planning, she had no intentions of teaching the way of the team members.

At Stromberg Elementary, 4th grade teachers collaborate, as a professional community, on different teaching methods and pedagogical strategies for the success of student learning. In sharing her lesson planning for 4th grade math with Mrs. Struppe, Mrs. Staunton disclosed technology integration and using learning stations to support differentiation were both important strategies expected by the 4th grade teachers and administration.

Mrs. Struppe explained that current trends made her work too "hard" and that she would continue teaching the way that she's always been teaching. Her exact words were, "I get a 100% every year and I see no reason to change anything." Since Mrs. Wolverton mandated that the teachers incorporate technology in their lesson plans and teaching methods, Mrs. Staunton tried speaking with Mrs. Struppe privately. Mrs. Staunton advised that Mrs. Wolverton and Mr. Perrault, the assistant principal, would begin spot-checking classrooms through walkthroughs to observe if teachers were following initiatives.

The walkthrough is a standard administrative practice that building administrators and instructional leaders and coaches used to improve instructional practices of teachers. The walkthrough enables the administrator or responsible party to obtain a snapshot of instructional and curricular practices. This is particularly germane when the building administration has implemented plans for improvement. The walkthrough is not intended for formal teacher evaluation purposes, but is focused on identifying what is missing in teaching and learning and serves as an opportunity to provide formative feedback to improve teaching practice. The purpose is to identify specific elements of instruction or principles of learning, collectively between the principal or instructional coach, and work to further improve classroom practices (Protheroe, 2009).

Mrs. Staunton also reminded Mrs. Struppe that she should participate in small group teaching as a way of differentiating instruction for struggling students. After all, this was an expectation set by the administration. Mrs. Struppe's adamant reply was that "small group teaching was the math specialist's and interventionist's jobs." This comment raised a concern for Mrs. Staunton with respect to Mrs. Struppe's teaching philosophy and her classroom practices. Wasn't Mrs. Struppe concerned with administrator expectations and with meeting the instructional needs of all students?

Throughout the year, Mrs. Staunton spoke with several individuals, including the math specialist, Mrs. Nettleton, about Mrs. Struppe's behavior, not disclosing the teachers' name. Mrs. Nettleton listened to Mrs. Staunton's concerns, noting she would be attentive to any teacher seeking assistance. Mrs. Staunton's justification in speaking with Mrs. Nettleton was that her students were not being supplied with equitable instruction. Mrs. Staunton was careful not to implicate Mrs. Struppe by name or accuse her of any practice that violated school policy or accepted practice.

Shortly after, Mrs. Nettleton began visiting math classrooms, including Mrs. Struppe's, and began documentation. Subsequently, the math specialist met with Mrs. Staunton to discuss her concerns that Mrs. Struppe was not providing qualified instruction to students as directed by district and school policy.

The question of what constituted qualified instruction was raised and Mrs. Nettleton and Mrs. Staunton shared a similar belief: It is the teacher's responsibility to serve all students in a fair and professional manner that is in accordance with district and school policy concerning teaching practices. There was brief mention of teacher ethics and a concern that Mrs. Struppe may be drifting away from expected ethical teaching practices, mainly "do no harm to students."

Several days later, Mrs. Struppe went to Mrs. Staunton and asked if she could copy Mrs. Staunton's small group documentation in order to duplicate it for her students. This seemed strange to Mrs. Staunton since Mrs. Struppe had previously stated that small group teaching wasn't her job. Duplicating the documentation for Mrs. Struppe's students wouldn't serve the needs of the students. Nevertheless, Mrs. Struppe was to be observed soon by building administration, and she explained the documentation was needed in her small group binder.

While the documentation wouldn't serve the needs of Mrs. Struppe's students it would serve Mrs. Struppe's need to pass the administrative observation. The question in Mrs. Staunton's mind was, isn't this unethical and how would using another teacher's documentation pass administrative observation?

Upon reflection, Mrs. Staunton perceived Mrs. Struppe's request was disingenuous given Mrs. Struppe's earlier comments concerning small group teaching and that it was the "math specialist's and interventionist's jobs." Mrs. Staunton elected to decline her request; she didn't feel comfortable in allowing Mrs. Struppe to use documentation for her class so that Mrs. Struppe would have some evidence of documentation, regardless that it would not be authentic.

During the following week, when checking her small group binders, Mrs. Staunton noticed that a student's documentation was missing from her small group math binder. Since Mrs. Staunton tracked the students' progress every week, she knew that information was organized accordingly and should not be missing; she carefully placed the documentation in each folder.

While the thought occurred that Mrs. Struppe may have taken the documentation, Mrs. Staunton didn't ask Mrs. Struppe if she'd seen the documentation; however, Mrs. Staunton did document that her small group binder had been tampered with, but she did not report the missing information to the school administration.

Mrs. Staunton's decision not to report the situation to Mrs. Wolverton or Mr. Perrault was due to her concern that Mrs. Wolverton had hired Mrs. Struppe and she was not comfortable about the relationship between Mrs. Wolverton and Mrs. Struppe; she was concerned about how reporting her suspicions might be received by Mrs. Wolverton. After all, it was only a suspicion but there was no evidence to suggest responsibility at the time. Mrs. Staunton decided to speak with Mrs. Nettleton, the math specialist about the missing information.

Several days later, the Mrs. Nettleton brought Mrs. Staunton her missing small group binder documentation. Mrs. Nettleton didn't disclose from where she had retrieved the documents. While it was comforting to have the documentation retrieved, it was disconcerting to Mrs. Staunton that the documents had been taken and she did not know by whom, although she had her suspicions.

During the next few months, scheduled administrator walkthroughs increased. First, Mrs. Staunton's classroom received a visit by Mrs. Wolverton. She noticed that attention was given to weekly objectives. Since Mrs. Staunton had a working understanding of administrator practices based on her tenure at Stromberg Elementary, she knew that the visits were focused on teaching strategies and whether or not the lessons were aligned with lesson plans and district objectives. Next, the administrators would go to each math teacher's class to observe.

Mrs. Staunton was sensitive that Mrs. Wolverton chose to conduct many, if not most of the walkthroughs but that she did not do so in Mrs. Struppe's classroom, rather Mr. Perrault conducted this walkthrough. Mrs. Staunton reflected once again on Mrs. Struppe's comment about technology and small group teaching and the missing documentation from her small group binder, wondering what Mr. Perrault observed when he visited Mrs. Struppe's classroom, and whether all was in order as is should be.

During regularly scheduled data team meetings, the administration would remind teachers of their expectations when observing each classroom during the walkthrough. Data teams are small grade-level or department teams that examine individual student work generated from common formative assessments. These teams are collaborative in nature, following structured, scheduled meetings that focus on effectiveness of teaching and learning. They generally have a team leader that facilitates and coordinates the team's work with formative assessment. Data teams align their work with the needs of all students and with the district and school policies and procedures concerning teaching practices (Ainsworth & Viegut, 2006; Perry, 2011; White, 2008).

The teachers would discuss student assessment progress and identify strategies to help struggling students. For the most part, teachers were collaborating and sharing ideas, except Mrs. Struppe who elected not to actively participate. However, in reflection over the course of weeks and months,

Mrs. Staunton always noticed that Mrs. Struppe's class never failed anything; in fact, her students always had the highest grades on any test. How could this be?

All 4th grade teachers became disturbed because they knew what Mrs. Struppe's students were capable of, and that when they taught them in focused small groups, they had no idea of the skills that the other teachers taught. During this time, Mrs. Fanning, the school counselor, who also served as testing coordinator for Stromberg Elementary, shared with Mrs. Staunton that several parents had contacted her with their concerns about how their children were being prepared for the "test" in Mrs. Struppe's classroom, but that other teachers were not following the same teaching practices.

The parents were concerned for their children. This raised another red flag for Mrs. Staunton, yet she elected not to voice this concern at the time with the principal, Mrs. Wolverton.

As data team leader, Mrs. Staunton approached Mrs. Struppe and asked her to share some of her strategies with the 4th grade team. Mrs. Struppe then disclosed that she "taught the skills that were going to be on the test and that she used old state standardized tests to teach test strategies. She didn't believe in teaching students unnecessary objectives when they wouldn't even use them in fourth grade." Mrs. Staunton did not have a response for what she had just heard. Mrs. Staunton reminded Mrs. Struppe of her ethical responsibilities as a teacher.

Mrs. Struppe told Mrs. Staunton that, "Mrs. Wolverton knew of the teaching strategies she used; that's why she was hired. That's why the principal always moved her, year to year, so that she could teach her son. She saw no reason to change if the principal didn't have a problem with her teaching methods." Mrs. Staunton thanked Mrs. Struppe for her time and ended the conversation. The fact that Mrs. Struppe openly shared this information about why she was hired by Mrs. Wolverton confirmed some of Mrs. Staunton's concerns about openly sharing with the principal any information related to Mrs. Struppe's behavior.

Mrs. Staunton spoke with Mrs. Nettleton, the math specialist, on the issue concerning Mrs. Struppe teaching the skills that were on the test using old TAKS tests. She also raised the question of teaching from old TAKS tests, and providing students with an advantage to scoring higher. Mrs. Staunton questioned if this was ethical and fair, wondering why the administration would condone this type of practice. Mrs. Nettleton told Mrs. Staunton that it was best for her to "keep her mouth shut because Mrs. Wolverton didn't want her or anyone messing up anything."

They discussed Mrs. Wolverton's aggressive strategies for increasing student growth and that Mrs. Wolverton didn't care how the scores increased as long as they increased. They also discussed Mrs. Wolverton's conduct of hiring a teacher and moving that teacher each year to follow her son's movement from one grade level to the next. The undertone of unethical practice was woven throughout the conversation.

When parents of students in Mrs. Struppe's class asked Mrs. Staunton what types of additional help they could get for their children, Mrs. Staunton offered them additional help, but did not disclose any information when the parents prompted Mrs. Staunton why their students did not know what other 4th grade students knew. Mrs. Staunton always referred them back to Mrs. Struppe.

At the end of every year, Mrs. Struppe's class always scored a 100% in everything. It was also disclosed that Mrs. Struppe continued to be the highest paid teacher in terms of teacher District Awards for Teacher Excellence (DATE) grants on the entire campus. Every parent requested that their child be placed in her class, and the office was forced to fill her classroom first.

DATE grants have been implemented in Texas schools as an incentive for teachers to improve standardized test scores. The intent was to reward teachers for high quality instruction. As currently configured, the DATE program could allow districts to create incentive programs that actually exacerbated rather than ameliorated inequities in the distribution of teacher quality. Many times the DATE grant becomes a form of compensation for encouraging teachers to follow directives that are of questionable ethical nature (Fuller, 2010).

However, it was collectively known that Mrs. Struppe also was assigned the highest ability students. Any students with special needs were not placed in her class. This posed another level of ethical concern on the part of teachers who were not favored in the same way. The inequity of student placement was a conversation that teachers shared but never in the presence of Mrs. Wolverton or Mr. Perrault.

The New Principal

The dynamics changed for Mrs. Struppe the following year. While there was no public discussion, Mrs. Wolverton left Stromberg Elementary School as principal. During the summer, Mrs. Manville replaced Mrs. Wolverton as principal. Mrs. Manville was more objective, she had no personal or political connections to the campus, nor, to any of the personnel hired by Mrs. Wolverton. Mrs. Manville was perceived as strict and at times a micromanager in terms of adherence to her requirements for classroom instruction.

As the year progressed Mrs. Struppe's teaching practice and her high scores on the state standardized test began to slip as she was increasingly forced to teach students of various capabilities, not just the highest ability students. The assignment of select students to her classroom was discontinued by Mrs. Manville, and Mrs. Struppe found her classroom more aligned with the classrooms of other teachers. She was also required to teach 4th grade objectives, although it seemed that she continued to find ways around teaching by using old TAKS tests when Mrs. Manville or Mr. Perrault were not observing or conducting walkthroughs in the classrooms.

Interestingly, Mr. Perrault was now more aligned with Mrs. Manville and his walkthroughs were more consistent and Mrs. Struppe was held more accountable in her methods. The new principal required documentation every week and both she and Mr. Perrault visited the classrooms regularly to ensure that small group instruction was observed. Over the next several weeks and months, more of Mrs. Staunton's students' small group math documentation began missing and Mrs. Staunton would simply ask Struppe to give them back. Several times, Mrs. Struppe personally asked Mrs. Staunton to teach her a particular skill so that she could in turn teach it to her students.

While the level of trust was very low on the part of Mrs. Staunton in terms of believing Mrs. Struppe truly wanted to improve her teaching practices, as a concerned professional, Mrs. Staunton agreed and provided professional assistance for Mrs. Struppe to understand the skills and strategies necessary for meeting the needs of the students. Mrs. Staunton's justification was that if Mrs. Struppe was provided with the knowledge and strategies, perhaps then she could begin teaching her students more than just the skills students need to know to pass a standardized test.

Teaching all students, not just the students of the highest abilities, was and continued to be a challenge for Mrs. Struppe. With Mrs. Manville replacing Mrs. Wolverton as principal, the first step in correcting a political positioning of a teacher to benefit selected students was addressed. It was also a first step in addressing unethical behavior on the part of a teacher, albeit, not the only step required to create a more ethical learning environment for all students.

THE LITERATURE REVIEW

Teachers in many countries today are faced with the complex and demanding nature of the worldwide proliferation of large-scale testing, a phenomenon that dates to the 1990s and has escalated in recent years (Pope et al., 2009). Standardized testing, as part of an educational agenda for accountability, has introduced new tensions into the classroom and school culture, presenting challenges and demands for both teachers and principals.

Teaching strategies and pedagogical practices often turn to preparing students for taking the test, moving away from teaching skills and knowledge necessary to being successful as the students matriculate through the educational system. Teachers are held accountable for test scores and often find themselves in difficult situations where the principal expects the teacher to "do what it takes" to ensure that high scores are obtained (Eastwood & Welsh, 2009).

The responsibility of teachers in terms of teaching all students is often juxtaposed with external (parental) and internal (administrative) and these demands create tensions for teachers, tensions that may direct the teacher to drift ethically in their practice, crossing professional boundaries of teaching practice motivated by self gain or political allegiance, and thus, creating breaches of conduct and behavior that affect students, colleagues, and parents (Johnson et al., 2008).

ETHICAL TEST PREPARATION

Many well-documented test-preparation practices essentially falsify test scores in order to create the appearance "that more learning has happened than was the case" (Haladyna, 2006, p. 37). Unethical test practices related to satisfying accountability requirements are the most pernicious, which result from imposed pressures to maintain high test scores. There is a distinction between ethical violations and legal violations, with unethical practices often leading to legal action including loss of position and professional certificate. A code of ethics is important to an educator's understanding of permissible practices.

EDUCATOR CODE OF ETHICS

Public schooling, and therein, testing and assessment practices takes a very different form within the United States and across other countries. Each state or nation-state has some form of a code of ethics to guide professional behavior and ethical conduct (Black & Wiliam, 2005; Pope et al., 2008; Shapira-Lishchinsky, 2011). An educator code of ethics is a set of normative standards of professional behavior that are intended to ensure that educators act in a professional and ethically responsible manner.

The code of ethics, in this sense, is premised on shared, normative principles accepted by the education profession. This may be at the state, federal, or institutional level, such as professional organizations or accreditation entities. For this reason, an unethical procedure or conduct in one area of a geographic region cannot logically be ethical under the same circumstances in another area. This is even more apparent when considering ethics on a global level between nation-states.

For the same reason, the wide extent of an unethical practice does not make it ethical or ethically acceptable. Educators are responsible for identifying the code of ethics that applies in their respective state, country, as well as

Ethical Practices in Preparing Students

Ethical test preparation practices are critically important (Johnson et al., 2008; Shapira-Lishchinsky, 2011). Principles of ethical standardized testing practices are concerned with raising educators' awareness, individually and collectively, and maintaining a high level of professional and ethical conduct in testing practices. The most ethical test preparation is good teaching: using the content standards, aligning instruction to these standards, assessing learning, reteaching, and reassessing. The teacher follows all content standards for the grade level and aligns instruction and assessment with that content (Welsh et al., 2014).

Examples of questionable and/or unethical test preparation practices include but are not limited to:

- Teaching to the test or coaching students on a test item in any manner prior to the test. This includes teaching or coaching during the school day or through homework assignments, relaying a memorized test item, making a list of most items used on a test, or copying manually or mechanically the actual test items.
- Using or giving students a test item from any part of the standardized test in which only a word, phrase, or distracter has been changed.
- Constructing or using any practice form that is similar to the actual test items to reflect the situations, options, or conditions of the original question can destroy item security and validity.
- Copying or distributing the standardized test or selected test items.
- Using old versions or used test forms from a mandated standardized testing program as practice materials (Colnerud, 2006; Haladyna, Nolen, & Haas, 1991; Pope et al., 2009; Popham, 2009; Welsh, Eastwood, & D'Agostino, 2014).

Ethical test preparation is predicated on the ethical character of educators to act in a professional and ethically responsible manner at all times. When an educator drifts across the ethical boundary in his or her practice, students are often the first to be harmed. This is particularly true in matters of standardized testing.

Ethical Practices of Campus Leaders

A genuine regard for students' best interests emerges as a major influence on principal leadership practices. Authentic leadership reflects ethical practices guided by the leaders' self-knowledge, sensitivity to ethical tensions, and a technical sophistication that leads to a synergy of leadership action (Begley, 2006). Principals and other campus leaders concerned with the consequences of their decisions and actions take direction from their values and valuation processes (Stefkovich & Begley, 2007).

Leaders should know their own values and ethical predispositions, as well as be sensitive to the value orientations of others. The valuation processes relate to leadership practices as a guide to action, particularly as supports to resolving ethical dilemmas (Begley & Johansson, 1998). Begley and Stefkovich (2007) explained that ethics, "in their purest forms tend to be expressed in a relatively context-stripped form that conveys the essence of the normative behavior" (p. 400).

Importantly, ethics are culturally derived norms, and therefore, ethical practices of leaders are culturally normative (Begley & Johansson, 1998). In this sense, ethical leadership practices are enacted in schools that are culturally enriched environments; seldom are ethics or ethical practices experienced in their purest form.

Ethical practices concerning standardized testing in the contemporary educational setting present challenges for campus leaders. The ubiquitous press for accountability in educational decision-making characteristic of current educational systems and the politics and ideologies that direct those systems "generates an effect on how and when principals will employ ethics as guides to their professional decision making" (Stefkovich & Begley, 2007, p. 210). Because ethics are often interpreted in culturally exclusive ways, and when enacted as ethical practices they can be troublesome to "employ as guides to action in our increasingly culturally diverse schools and communities where administrators increasingly sense the need to be accountable for their decisions" (Stefkovich & Begley, 2007, p. 210).

Campus leaders "tend to consciously employ ethics as a guide to action relatively infrequently and under particular conditions" (Begley & Stefkovich, 2007, p. 401). Situations concerning high stakes testing and meeting standards for accountability are examples when ethical dilemmas present difficult challenges for leaders, particularly depending on the tensions caused by reporting of campus ratings and low test scores.

Increasingly, standardized testing and demands of accountability result in unethical testing practices. Examples of unethical practices include:

1. Allowing and encouraging students to be absent the day of testing;
2. Directing teachers to engage in unethical practices concerning test preparation;
3. Grouping students to ensure high test scores for selected populations;
4. Subverting school/district policy and procedure to allow for instructional methods that are unethical;

5. Making secure test items or modified secure test items available to teachers for instruction (teaching to the test);
6. Allowing or requiring test administrators to change student responses;
7. Reclassifying students solely for the purpose of avoiding state testing;
8. Not testing all eligible students;
9. Failing to provide needed modifications during testing, if available;
10. Modifying scoring programs including answer keys, equating files, and lookup tables;
11. Modifying student records solely for the purpose of raising test scores; and
12. Misleading the public concerning the results and interpretations of test data.

The term "best interests" is frequently used by educators and policy makers when discussing professional and ethical practice, in particular concerning students. "School leaders tend to interpret this phrase in a variety of ways, often times disagreeing on the best course of action, and what is truly in the best interests of the student" (Stefkovich & Begley, 2007, p. 401).

The "best interest" of students is a campus leader's responsibility and determining the "best interest" of students goes hand-in-hand with "do no harm" to students when making ethical decisions concerning standardized testing.

ETHICAL RESPONSIBILITY OF TEACHERS

Teachers deal with many varied ethical situations in their daily practice (Colnerud, 1997, 2006). They encounter issues, such as inappropriate allocation of resources, principals' hiring practices, allowances for teacher practices that create inequities, and irresponsible colleagues. Shapira-Lishchinsky (2011) noted that when the teachers' "sense of proper action is constrained by complex factors in educational practice and decisions are made and carried out contrary to the 'right course'...ethical conflict and moral distress result" and an ethical dilemma arises (p. 648).

Ethical Dilemmas in Teaching

An ethical dilemma is explained as "a circumstance that requires a choice between competing sets of principles in a given, usually undesirable or perplexing, situation (Cranston, Ehrich, & Kimber, 2003, p. 137). The dilemma is represented by choices between two or more possible courses of action on the part of the teacher.

Shapira-Lishchinsky (2011) provided an example, between loyalty to colleagues and school norms, noting that teachers "are expected to act in accordance with professional ethics. Teachers sometimes witness a colleague mistreating a pupil, or are informed of such mistreatment that is not in line with school norms, and find it difficult to confront the colleague" (p. 649).

Professional ethics, Husu (2001) explained, "concerns the norms, values, and principles that should govern the conduct of educational professionals" (p. 68). Professional ethics connotes ethical behavior. When confronted with an ethical dilemma, a teacher must make a choice, sometimes a choice that may determine the future of his or her professional career.

Green, Johnson, Kim, and Pope (2007) define ethical behavior as acting based on one's judgment of an obligation—a duty by virtue of a relationship with a person, persons, or social institution; in the case of teaching, a relationship between teacher and student, teacher and colleagues, teacher and principal, or teacher and parent. Ethical dilemmas are complex problems that present conflict between values and beliefs of individuals. Ethical dilemmas require the teacher to act ethically. "What makes a behavior ethical or unethical is whether that behavior is consistent with or contradictory to one's obligations" (Green et al., 2007, p. 1000).

Ethical Responsibilities for Teachers in Standardized Testing

Concerning standardized testing and classroom assessment practices, there are two primary ethical responsibilities of educators. First, because assessment can significantly affect students, the ethical responsibility of educators is "first, do no harm" (Taylor & Nolen, 2005 p. 7). Ethically responsible behavior is defined as acting based on one's judgment of an obligation, ethical in nature and to students first and foremost. In addition, the notion of an ever-present gap between principles and ethical behavior in specific circumstances requires a focus on specific judgments as well as on general principles, such as do no harm.

As Green et al. (2007) explained, at times, the principle of do no harm emerges as a dilemma in practice, as a choice between two or more harms. "A teacher may have to choose between a high-stakes exam that yields important data about student performance and the emotional stress that such exams cause in students (and teachers)" (pp. 1009-1010). This dilemma (the choice between harms) is seen as "potentially more 'normal' than the avoidance of harm altogether" (p. 1010).

A second general guiding principle for standardized testing and classroom assessment is to avoid score pollution (see Popham, 1991, 2000; Haladyna, 2006). Score pollution is any practice that improves test performance without concurrently increasing actual mastery of the content tested. "Teaching to the test is a ubiquitous term often defined as decontextualized instruction intended to artificially inflate test scores" (Welsh, Eastwood, & D'Agostino, 2014, p. 98).

Teaching to the test, such as using an older version of a standardized achievement test, is a form of score pollution in that the score on the test does not represent actual student achievement in the content area. Haladyna (2006) explained that any "test is only a sample from a large domain of knowledge and skills; mastering a small part of the domain that happens to be tested creates a biased test score" (p. 37). Green et al. (2007) further explained that "the score on the test does not represent actual student achievement in the content area and is 'polluted' by factors unrelated to academic attainment. If scores do not reflect mastery then harm has been done" (p. 1001).

Ethical Responsibilities for Campus Leaders

Campus leaders are responsible for compliance with standard practices and ethical conduct toward students, professional colleagues, school officials, parents, and members of the community and shall safeguard academic freedom (TEA, 2010). Ethical responsibilities include hiring personnel for a position directly related to standardized test administration (i.e., classroom teachers), monitoring all practices related to standardized testing, adhering to performance appraisal of personnel, assuring all teachers follow standards for curriculum and instruction and assessment, addressing policy and procedures related to teaching and testing, and ensuring that all campus leaders and personnel adhere to professional codes of conduct at all times (Campbell, 2003; Starratt, 2004).

As campus leader, the principal, and his or her administrative team, holds a position of public trust (Kochan & Reed, 2005) and therein is held accountable for the success of all students; the measure of success is determined by the progress of each student toward realization of his or her potential (TEA, 2010). A breach of ethical conduct is violation of public trust on the part of a campus leader and it places individuals at risk, students, teachers, parents, and all parties vested in the public school. Principals are ethically responsible and morally accountable for leading the school (Ehrich, 2000).

A breach of ethical conduct is an act of intentionally and knowingly violating a professional and/or statutory code of ethics established by a state or nation-state or licensing or certificating organization (Starratt, 2004; TEA, 2010). When the principal or members of his administrative team acts intentionally, that is, he or she makes a decision or takes action, with respect to the nature of his or her ethical and professional conduct that results in harm to others, the campus leader has acted in a manner deemed unethical (TEA, 2010; Tenbrunsel & Messick, 2004).

Hiring personnel to fill a teaching position, which directly benefits the principal (i.e., to ensure high test scores for the principal's own child, regardless of the cost or harm to students), is an example of ethical fading (Tenbrunsel & Messick, 2004), that is, loosing sight of or disregarding one's ethical responsibilities. Ethical fading on the part of the principal as campus leader is his or her conscious objective or desire to engage in the conduct or cause a result that is perceived as a breach of ethical responsibility and which disadvantages some (students and teachers) while benefiting a select few or one (high performing students or the principal's child).

The campus leader's ethical responsibility is to all students, teachers, parents, and community members. Public trust is fragile and easily broken. Once broken public trust is very difficult to regain, both for those individuals currently holding the position of campus leader and for those individuals who will follow in that role.

When a principal or members of his or her administrative team acts knowingly, or with knowledge, in making decisions or taking actions, and he or she is aware of the nature of the conduct that does meet the measure of ethical responsibility or that the circumstances exist, and that conduct knowingly violates the "do no harm" rule, then the campus leader has broken with public trust and has violated his or her professional code of ethics (Kochan & Reed, 2005).

CONCLUSION

The emphasis on standardized testing inevitably raises issues related to ethical concerns as practices evolve; ethical dilemmas emerge as teachers are confronted with demands on higher test scores and maintaining a school rating that reflects well on the district. The ethical dilemmas associated with teaching and standardized testing illuminate the complexity of the teaching profession and the uncertainty and ambiguity that accompany the discussion of ethical practices in education. Standardized testing creates a unique tension in the school culture that may cause otherwise ethical educators to drift across boundaries into unethical conduct.

THE GUIDING QUESTIONS

The following questions are presented to help you think critically about the case study. Answer them by using your own state, federal, professional codes, policies, and laws. Standardized testing has created many challenges for educators. Certainly teaching practices are a focal point discourse and concern at the local, state, national, and global levels.

1. What are the defining factors that led to the ethical dilemma presented in the case study?

2. Who is primarily responsible for creating the dilemma and how could the person or persons have prevented the conflict leading to the dilemma?
3. Concerning "do no harm" and "avoid score pollution" as two points of ethical responsibility for educators, who are the responsible parties and what should be done?
4. Do you believe that Mrs. Struppe acted ethically in the case? Consider her actions and explain at what points in the case study you perceive that she acted unethically and/or should have acted differently.
5. Do you believe that Mrs. Staunton acted ethically in the case? Consider her actions and explain at what points in the case study you perceive that she acted ethically and/or should have acted differently.
6. Do you believe the administration acted ethically in the case? Consider Mrs. Wolverton and Mr. Perrault's actions and explain at what points in the case study you perceive that they acted ethically and/or should have acted differently. The Educator Code of Ethics is a set of normative standards to guide professional behavior and serve as a safeguard against unlawful actions on the part of educators.
7. Review your Educator Code of Ethics. Drawing from the Code of Ethics, what specific ethical standards do you find that are applicable to the case study?
8. Examining the case study, in particular Mrs. Struppe and Mrs. Wolverton's actions concerning standardized test practices, what does your Code of Ethics establish, specifically, about standardized testing?
9. Based again on the Code of Ethics, what course of action should be taken with Mrs. Struppe, Mrs. Wolverton, Mr. Perrault, and Mrs. Staunton, if any?

FINAL CONSIDERATIONS

In retrospect, the nature of the problems presented in the case are complex, more so than one might first surmise. The ethical breach of conduct on the part of school administrators and teachers requires discussion of the ethical and moral character of the individuals. However, the depth of attention needed in this case calls into question the supervision of building principals, which reflects on the upper administration and its responsibility to hold school level personnel accountable to district and state policy, as well as legal and ethical standards.

Oversight of decision making at the building level, in terms of the principal's actions and decisions, draws into question a level of responsibility to the upper administration, in this case the superintendent and central office personnel. The question that must be addressed is what level of oversight is in place and the degree with which oversight is addressed?

Specifically, the importance of hiring personnel at the building level, in this case, hiring a teacher with specific directives to prepare select students for standardized testing success draws the entire administration into question in terms of oversight of hiring practices and it questions the need for additional policy/procedure that ensures all personnel are meeting not only policy directives, but equally important, that they are meeting ethical and legal standards as well. The question that must be addressed is whether district policy/procedure has sufficient safeguards?

Standardized testing introduces an external force into the educational setting, a force that mandates a level of accountability on the part the school. Importantly, securing and maintaining public trust is a primary responsibility of the school district, from the teacher in the classroom to the building principal to the superintendent. Addressing mandated accountability, standards, and testing in schools is a complex responsibility that calls into question public trust in district personnel. The question that must be addressed is what assurances are in place that all district personnel work to understand and maintain public trust?

In the case of Maleficent Independent School District and the ethical dilemma created by the personnel in Stromberg Elementary, the district has the primary responsibility for all its personnel, and therefore, the district has the responsibility for setting and maintaining high standards of ethical, as well as legal practices. In this case, it was necessary, on the part of the superintendent and central office, to evaluate the principal's hiring practices and to substantiate that the principal was following district policy and procedure. The question that must be addressed is what procedures are in play that assures that all human behavior is adjudicated appropriately and morally?

The teachers involved in the case also have an ethical responsibility to the students, parents, to their colleagues, and to the district to address improprieties with respect to differentiating and assigning students to teachers, maintaining proper classroom records, following pedagogical practices, and appropriate test preparation procedures, as well as building level practices that harm and/or discriminate against students. The question that must be addressed is whether "do no harm" is meaningfully implemented?

School personnel are responsible for ascertaining what the school and district level policies/procedures are, and, in turn, understanding, as well as discerning the correct and incorrect interpretation of policy/procedure. In matters of hiring or standardized testing practices, the distance between ethical and legal is the attention to policy/procedure and the difference between acting/decision making on behalf of the public versus on behalf of self-serving actions and decisions that compromise the integrity of personnel and erode public trust. The question that must be addressed is whether one is acting in the best interest of others or him or herself?

REFERENCES

Ainsworth, L., & Viegut, D. (2006). *Common formative assessments: How to connect standards-based instruction and assessment*. Thousand Oaks, CA: Corwin Press.

Airasian, P. (2005). *Assessment in the classroom: A concise approach* (2nd ed.). Boston, MA: McGraw-Hill Company.

Begley, P. T. (2006). Self-knowledge, capacity and sensitivity: Prerequisites to authentic leadership by school principals. *Journal of Educational Administration, 44*(6), 570-589.

Begley, P. T., & Johansson, O. (1998). The values of school administration: Preferences, ethics and conflicts. *Journal of School Leadership, 8*(4), 399-422.

Begley, P. T., & Stefkovich, J. (2007). Integrating values and ethics into post secondary teaching for leadership development: Principles, concepts, and strategies. *Journal of Educational Administration, 45*(4), 398-412.

Black, P., & Wiliam, D. (2005). Lessons from around the world: How policies, politics and cultures constrain and afford assessment practices. *The Curriculum Journal, 16*(2), 249-261.

Campbell, E. (2003). Let right be done: Trying to put ethical standards into practice. In P. T. Begley and O. Johansson (Eds.), *The ethical dimensions of school leadership* (pp. 107-125). Dordrecht: Kluwer Academic Publishers.

Colnerud, G. (1997). Ethical conflicts in teaching. *Teaching and Teacher Education, 13*, 627-635.

Colnerud, G. (2006). Teacher ethics as a research problem syntheses achieved and new issues. *Teachers and Teaching: Theory and Practice, 12*(3), 365-385.

Cranston, N., Ehrich, L., & Kimber, M. (2005). Ethical dilemmas: The "bread and butter" of educational leaders' lives. *Journal of Educational Administration, 44*(2), 106-121.

Eastwood, M., & Welsh, M. E. (2009). *Do states inadvertently encourage "teaching to the test"?* Paper presented at the annual meeting of the Northeast Educational Research Association, Rocky Hill, CT.

Ehrich, L. (2000). Principals as morally accountable leaders. *International Journal of Education Reform, 9*(2), 120-127.

Fuller, E. (2010). *Study of the distribution of teacher quality in Texas schools*. Austin, TX: The Association of Texas Professional Educators.

Green, S. K., Johnson, R. L., Kim, D.-H., & Pope, N. S. (2007). Ethics in classroom assessment practices: Issues and attitudes. *Teaching and Teacher Education, 23*, 999-1011.

Haladyna, T. M. (2006). Perils of standardized achievement testing. *Educational Horizons, 85*(1), 30-43.

Haladyna, T. M., Nolen, S. B., & Haas, N. S. (1991). Raising standardized achievement test scores and the origins of test score pollution. Educational Researcher, 20(5), 2-7.

Husu, J. (2001). Teachers at cross-purposes: A case-report approach to the study of ethical dilemmas in teaching. *Journal of Curriculum and Supervision, 17*(1), 67-89.

Johnson, R., Green, S., Kim, D., & Pope, N. (2008). Educational leaders' perceptions about ethical assessment practices. *The American Journal of Evaluation, 29*, 520-530.

Kochan, F. K., & Reed, C. J. (2005). Collaborative leadership, community building, and democracy in public education. In F. W. English (Ed.), *The Sage handbook of educational leadership: Advances in theory, research, and practice* (pp. 68-84). Thousand Oaks, CA: Sage Publications, Inc.

Perry, A. (2011). *The data teams experience: A guide for effective meetings*. Englewood, CO: Lead & Learn Press.

Pope, N., Green, S. K., Johnson, R. L., & Mitchell, M. (2008). Examining teacher ethical dilemmas in classroom assessment. *Teacher and Teacher Education, 25*, 778-782.

Popham, W. J. (1991). Appropriateness of teachers' test-preparation practices. *Educational Measurement: Issues and Practice, 10*(4), 12-15.

Popham, W. J. (2000). *Modern educational measurement: Practical guidelines for educational leaders*. Needham, MA: Allyn & Bacon.
Popham, W. J. (2009). Assessment literacy for teachers: Faddish or fundamental? *Theory Into Practice, 48*, 4-11.
Protheroe, N. (2009). Using classroom walkthroughs to improve instruction. *Principal, 88*(4), 30-34.
Shapira-Lishchinsky, O. (2011). Teachers' critical incidents: Ethical dilemmas in teaching practice. *Teaching and Teacher Education, 27*(3), 648-656.
Starratt, R. J. (2004). *Ethical leadership*. San Francisco: Jossey-Bass.
Stefkovich, J., & Begley, P. T. (2007). Ethical school leadership: Defining the best interests of students. *Educational Management Administration & Leadership, 35*(2), 205-224.
Taylor, K., & Nolen, S. (2005). *Classroom assessment: Supporting teaching and learning in real classrooms*. Upper Saddle River, NJ: Pearson Education, Inc.
Tenbrunsel, A. E., & Messick, D. M. (2004). Ethical fading: The role of self-deception in unethical behavior. *Social Justice Review, 17*(2), 223-236.
Texas Educational Agency. (2010). *SECTION 247.2. Code of Ethics and Standard Practices for Texas Educators*. Retrieved from: http://txrules.elaws.us/rule/title19_chapter247_sec.247.2
Texas Educational Agency. (2015a). *Overview of the Academic Excellence Indicator System 1990-91 through 2011-2012*. Retrieved from: http://ritter.tea.state.tx.us/perfreport/aeis/about.aeis.html
Texas Educational Agency. (2015b). *Accountability Rating System for Texas Public Schools and Districts*. Retrieved from: http://ritter.tea.state.tx.us/perfreport/account/index.html
Welsh, M. E., Eastwood, M., & D'Agostino, J. V. (2014). Conceptualizing teaching to the test under standards-based reform. *Applied Measurement in Education, 27*, 98-114.
White, S. (2008). *Getting beyond the numbers to data teams work*. Englewood, CO: Leadership and Learning Center.

Chapter Eleven

Purpose, Processes, and Change

Issues Parents and Stakeholders Bring to Schools

Peggy Malone

The role of the principal is central to parents and stakeholders having input to the purpose and processes at school campuses. As the focus of education continues to broaden, the need for feedback from parents and community members is vital to enhance services and opportunities for all students. However, this feedback is not without issues as multiple perspectives are brought into schools daily.

THE CASE STUDY

The Changing Role of the Principal

As the new school year began, the energy of students and their eager parents filtered throughout the community of Lake Hollow. During the summer, the principal, Ms. Charbeneau, invested a great deal of time meeting with school and community focus groups to discuss an identified need for more time to be spent on relevant learning and less time spent on repetitive, formative assessments during the school day. After reviewing the charts and notes from these meetings, it was apparent that the key to success was a multiple perspective family engagement model, which touched all groups, represented at the school.

Luckily, Ms. Charbeneau had a halftime parent volunteer coordinator to assist in these efforts. However, there was so much work and so little time. In the past, parental or family involvement at Lake Hollow Middle School was dominated by scheduled meetings, discipline matters, or seeking financial assistance for projects at the school. However, as the Lake Hollow Middle School educators realized that parental involvement in education is of paramount importance and that parental involvement leads to better student performance, it was evident that more detailed work was needed in this area.

Being a former reading teacher, Ms. Charbeneau knew that an International Reading Association position statement endorsed the importance of working with students and family members to increase achievement. The position statement also provided evidence that family (parental) involvement in the education of students is critical to effective schooling, that it improves student achievement, attitudes toward learning, and self-esteem. It was also pointed out that schools encouraging such partnerships are more likely to produce students who perform better than identical schools that do not involve families (International Reading Association, 2003).

Campus Challenges

The challenge was how to effectively engage all stakeholders of the school. During the previous two school years, Lake Hollow Middle School had revisited the roles that parents can play and worked to find new ways to involve parents in the education of their children. These stakeholders were involved in setting the vision and mission statements and writing goals supporting the educational process.

With increased recommended formative assessment practices, teachers devised checklists, combined with teacher observation and portfolios, and monitored students' performance. Linked to this formative assessment, a conferencing component was added that requires parents to make regular visits to schools to participate in conferences with their children's teacher regarding their performance in the classroom. The underlying belief was that parents are experts on their children and possess a great deal of information that teachers do not have. These insights were useful in building educational programs that support student success.

The ability to communicate, organize, lead, and sustain multiple parent engagement which effectively connects the family to learning goals of individual students is a complex task. The art of community engagement is actually based on an integrated system designed to connect with all stakeholders. This year's challenge was much larger than the work completed in previous years. It was obvious that Lake Hollow Middle School was moving toward implementation of systematic and sustained efforts to integrate parents into the fabric of their schools.

To add mystery to the project, Ms. Charbeneau was the only campus principal willing to take on this monumental opportunity. The superintendent, Dr. Rairia, was complimentary and supportive of her efforts and thought this work held great promise for the students of Lake Hollow Community School District. *How could she deliver the needed family engagement opportunities in a connected and seamless manner to a diverse population of 750 middle school students, their parents, and caregivers?* This was the continuous message strumming Ms. Charbeneau's thoughts as she experienced the joys associated with her fourth year opening day at Lake Hollow Middle School.

Reflecting on Priorities and Next Steps

As she considered an approach to developing the initial plan, Principal Charbeneau began to reflect on issues that stakeholders brought to the campus during her tenure at Lake Hollow Middle School. It was obvious that the diversity of the community impacted the types of issues brought to her for guidance, review, and action. Many of the parents and families had high expectations for these children and felt that education was the path to a better life and college success.

Another group of stakeholders was most interested in the socialization aspect that schools contribute to the upbringing of students, and their areas of concern tended to be related to the purpose of education and processes, which promote civility and respect for others. However, there were also vocal stakeholders who demanded specific services for students that the structure or budget did not always allow for in these economically competitive times. Of course in each of these groups, there were politics, which impacted these individuals' issues and requests. Sadly, another group of stakeholders was continuing to grow at Lake Hollow Middle School: absent or not involved parents or family members.

This growing trend created the most concern, and Principal Charbeneau understood the complex issues which drove this isolated approach. Intense jobs, scarcity of resources, emotional deficits, lack of time and transportation, and abdication of the responsibility of education were just a few of the reasons for not being involved in their student's education. The new design for stakeholder engagement had to create paths of support for these community members. In order to design meaningful opportunities to recruit these absent parents back into their child's education, tough decisions had to be made and relevant data must be gathered. Yes, it was definitely going to be a challenge to effectively engage all stakeholders of Lake Hollow Middle School.

Collaborative Action

Follow-up discussions with campus faculty and staff led to categorically organizing these issues with supporting data into three areas: 1) purpose, 2) processes, and 3) changes in structures at the district or campus level. The preliminary design of the campus engagement for Lake Hollow Middle School began to shift from campus determined model to a model of dynamic, interconnected work full of living qualities (Jaworski, 1998). What an exciting year that it was going to be for the campus and its stakeholders. The project management framework located in Table 11.1, *Lake Hollow Issues Analysis Chart*, illustrates the campus template that campus stakeholders would use in categorizing issues at Lake Hollow Middle School.

THE LITERATURE REVIEW

Historically, education has been tasked with the opportunity to address a diverse array of societal expectations and challenges. These opportunities range from closing the gaps in student achievement, college preparation, career and workforce readiness, and instilling or reinforcing expected moral or civic values to instruction in healthy habits which fuel future life success. Social contexts in which students, teachers, administrators, parents, and community stakeholders interact create multiple causal issues, which influence educational processes and outcomes.

Focus Area	Typical Issues	Stakeholders Involved	Communication/Engagement
Purpose of Work			
Processes			
Structure Changes			

Table 11.1. Lake Hollow Issues Analysis Chart

The Focus

Three distinct themes can be created from prevalent issues stakeholders bring to the school environment: 1) the purpose and organizational structures of schools, 2) inequality and processes for the continued work of schools; and 3) changing familiar structures of schooling. Specific theories of change and education policies are foundational in efforts to advance equity and goals of society, and an examination of this information is necessary to understand the perspectives of involved education stakeholders.

Contributing Philosophers

Philosophers were instrumental in the thought development regarding the different purposes of education and schools. Socrates contributed a form of inquiry and discussion between individuals, based on asking and answering questions to stimulate critical thinking and to illuminate ideas and the Socratic method and continues to be used in educational settings throughout the world (Reed & Johnson, 1996). Aristotle was an early contributor to the belief systems of the purpose and organizational structures of schools. Aristotle's work reflects his belief system that the thinking and practice as educators must include a deep concern for the ethical and political needs which makes for flourishing humans. His belief was that we should work for that which is good or "right," not merely "correct" (Aristotle, trans. 1976).

Many of the philosophers placed importance on "balanced" development, which included play, music, debate, science, physical training, and philosophy. Aristotle also bequeathed to us the long-standing categorizing of disciplines into the theoretical, practical, and technical (Aristotle, trans. 1976).

Plato was the teacher of Aristotle, and one of the most influential figures in Western thought. The first university, his Academy, was founded near Athens around 385 BC. Plato's early dialogues use the Socratic method of questioning. The questioning of the expert by the searcher of knowledge often exposed gaps in the reasoning; thus, demonstrating Plato's dislike of a rhetoric teaching method and believed all teachers should know their subject (Reed & Johnson, 1996).

Contemporary Views on Education

Throughout modern times, philosophers have proposed systematic purposes of schooling in today's society. In 1938, John Dewey argued that the primary purpose of education and schooling is not so much to *prepare* students to live a useful life, but to teach them how to live pragmatically and *immediately* in their current environment (Dewey, 1916). To G.S. Counts, the purpose of school was less about preparing individuals to live independently and more about preparing individuals to live as members of a society (Counts, 1978).

In the 1980s, the noted educator and philosopher Mortimore Adler put forth the Paideia Proposal (Adler, 1982), which integrated the ideas of Dewey and Counts, as well as his own. Specifically, Adler suggested that there are three objectives of children's schooling:

- the development of citizenship,
- personal growth or self-improvement, and
- occupational preparation. (p. 11)

Historian of education David Tyack has argued that from an historical perspective, the purpose of schooling has been tied to social and economic needs (Tyack, 1988). More recently, deMarrais and LeCompte (1995) outlined four major purposes of schooling that include:

- intellectual purposes such as the development of mathematical and reading skills;
- political purposes such as the assimilation of immigrants;
- economic purposes such as job preparation; and
- social purposes such as the development of social and moral responsibility. (p. 29)

As institutions of formal education emerged specific types of educational processes gained prominence. Schooling has also been used in social selection, industrial policy, and reproduction of social, economic, and political structures. In some countries educational institutions have acquired a key role in reproducing social elites.

In Paul Willis's study, *Learning to Labour*, explicit and implicit educational curricula reproduced social class. The incentives for schooling were visible and relevant mainly for kids who did not come from working-class families. As a result, working-class kids learned to hate school, and happily repeated the life patterns of their relatively uneducated families (Willis, 1977). As time moved forward, the expectations of education expressed by parents and stakeholders created a longer list of challenges for schools to consider in their short- and long-term planning and daily instructional delivery.

Influence of Education on Culture

It has been written that educational systems fulfill important social functions through an integrating and socializing function and through cultural transfer. Society members speak the same language, obey the same explicit and implicit rules and routines, and share beliefs. The social world needs to be stable and predictable for us to operate in it (Tuomi & Miller, 2011).

Cultural transfer, the exchange of objects and ideas and their resulting reinterpretations, through education is an effective means to generate the stability required by the continuation of social life (Tuomi & Miller, 2011). Experience was central to John Dewey's educational philosophy and he wrote of the two principles of continuity and interaction as not being separate from each other. These intercept and unite as the longitudinal and lateral aspects of experience. Continuity and interaction in active union with each other provide the measure of the educative significance and value of an experience (Dewey, 1938).

In today's times, the purpose of schools focuses on student academic performance with a growing interest in college and career readiness performance. Additionally, Robinson (2015) stated that education has to be a human business to meet the economic demands of the 21st century or lead to the fulfillment of students' natural interests. Societal expectations from the communities of these schools heavily influence the purposes of today's schools.

Alongside these expectations, the contributions of parents, caregivers, and other stakeholders vary drastically in communities throughout the world. As a result, the challenges brought to the school campus reflect these multiple expectations of schools. Principal Charbeneau's work at Lake Hollow Middle School to analyze these challenges illustrates a first step in responding to these varying expectations. The educational expectations of of K-12 students are much different from those in previous centuries. In the next section, we'll examine how educational leaders can respond to these needs.

Meeting Student Needs in the 21st Century

The 21st century education enterprise is very different from previous centuries. Factors, such as educational technology, global competition, and educational entrepreneurs contributed to the changing face of education. Educators and educational stakeholders are collaborating to deliver education in new and different ways, but this is not without challenges. Research indicates three barriers that surround the restructuring of education:

1. reluctance of public school partners to partner with for-profit schools and companies;
2. cultural differences between nonprofits and for-profit schools; and
3. a struggle of businesses to communicate their value to public education institutions. These barriers are the foundation of inequality and disconnect among interdependent education stakeholders (Smith & Humberstone, 2015).

The hierarchal design of education creates a path for interdependence; however, a silo mentality in educational settings creates challenges for the continued work of schools. By recognizing the value of interdependence of traditional and nontraditional stakeholders, public and private stakeholders, K-12 and colleges or universities, different roles and operating cultures can be overcome (Smith & Humberstone, 2015). Differing cultures and lack of communication challenge these interdependent partnerships, but relationship building is an effective step toward addressing the barriers challenging education.

A current term used in describing products, such as Dropbox and Survey Monkey is "freemium model" which combines free (basic product) and premium (additional functionality and support). A "freemium" approach to designing educational delivery in schools' partners' nonprofit educational stakeholders and for-profit educational stakeholders to deliver more effective and efficient instructional delivery tools (Smith & Humberstone, 2015).

If education leaders do not have a relationship with these differing providers, the opportunity to deliver the best teaching and learning to students is missed. As a result, the ability of educational leaders, such as Principal Charbeneau, will be limited in meeting the academic challenges and expectations brought to today's schools. Access and equity are enhanced when interdependence is brought into the instructional planning and communication cycle. This was a goal in the work being done by the administration, faculty and staff at Lake Hollow Middle School.

Impact of Community in Today's Schools

As diversity in society increases and people exercise their rights to present and challenge issues, divergent views surface regarding the structure of schools. An incompatibility with these views creates functional or dysfunctional conflict. Functional conflict can be characterized by a win-win attitude and harmony while dysfunctional conflict is characterized by a win-lose attitude and hostility (Bacal & Associates, 2012).

The structure of schools is largely related to the community expectations and traditional values placed on the education process. Cultural transfer is occurring in this process. As the norms and expectations within society shift, the impact on education can be seen and felt. These norms and expectations impact the issues that parents and other stakeholders bring to schoolhouses throughout the world.

THE GUIDING QUESTIONS

These guiding questions are useful in connecting your specific experiences and knowledge to issues and challenges brought to schools today. As you work through these questions, it is important to reflect on the changing focus of education throughout the centuries.

1. Based on your experiences, what is the purpose of a middle school education from the perspective of the parents or caregiver, teacher, administrator, and student? How do you bridge differences in these multiple perspectives?
2. In what ways are your school's standards likely to improve with the involvement of parents in program planning and implementation?
3. What prerequisites are necessary for schools and parents to become involved meaningfully in partnering?
4. To what extent does the nature of the issue predict the quality and extent of partnerships in the educational environment?
5. Interest in philanthropic groups to fund parent-engagement efforts is on the rise. In what ways, could the principal, Ms. Charbeneau, mobilize this resource area?
6. The U.S. Department of Education released a family and community engagement model to encourage efforts directly linked to student learning in 2014. Additionally, a growing field of family engagement researchers continues to collect data and conduct research. Describe techniques Ms. Charbeneau could use to involve the school faculty and staff in becoming knowledgeable of these documents.
7. Design a timeline with specific implementation activities for the upcoming school year, which demonstrates a commitment to developing a systematic family engagement process, but allows time for group collaborative efforts and new learning.
8. What systems of communication are needed to support this systematic approach to family engagement presented in the case study?
9. Are there specific areas of professional development needed to support faculty, staff and families in these expectations?
10. Why does organizational health play an important role in the success of a new initiative, and how can a principal encourage adjustments as needed to this area?
11. Describe the profile of an educator that you know which would support the goals and expectations of this community and family engagement model described in the case study.

FINAL CONSIDERATIONS

Final considerations to the questions above are described below. It is important for campus leaders to keep focused on creating opportunities for all students while addressing issues impacting student achievement and campus culture. As you work through these questions, reflect on these final considerations to build your knowledge and skills of the purpose of education, processes to improve education, and potential issues brought to schools daily.

1. Middle school students are an interesting group due to the varying degrees of social, emotional, and academic development each student brings to the classroom setting. Thus, perspectives of a parent or caregiver may focus primarily on academic maturity and contributing to finding long-term areas of interest to support these academic goals. A teacher's and administrator's perspective typically supports this area of focus with additional emphasis on collaborating and giving back to their community. Additionally, the middle school years are the initial years that students can begin to explore academic and extracurricular areas of interest, and these activities are critical to the whole child development. The range of perspectives held by middle school students can create changes daily in their attitude and performance. Gaps can be bridged by schools providing a quality curriculum focused on individual need and interest areas. Additionally, instruction in the classroom should be delivered in multiple formats to support learner differences and multiple perspectives of the role of education in today's societies. Structure with flexibility describes this organizational approach to middle school needs and the varying perspectives of parents or caregivers, teachers, administrators, and middle school students.
2. The involvement of parents, caregivers and community members impact school standards through an input process that promotes teaching and learning reflective of the expectations of all stakeholders. The dialogue created during the program planning process fosters pathways for deeper understanding of educational expectations and needs, as well as an interpretation of the campus role in the development of middle school students. Through these planning sessions, ideas are shared and combined to strengthen school standards and opportunities for increased teaching and learning performance.
3. Prerequisites for schools and parents to become meaningfully in partnership activities is the ability to listen to the heart, as well as with the mind. An understanding of state expectations and any approved flexibility through the state education agency is also an important prerequisite for meaningful partnerships. A commitment to listen actively and seek best opportunities for all students creates a strong foundation for effective partnerships. Ground rules for discussions and partnership work should also be included as a prerequisite tool to minimize negative behavior during passionate planning discussions.

REFERENCES

Adler, M. J. (1982). *The Paidea proposal: An educational manifesto.* New York: Collier Macmillian.

Aristotle, Thomson, J. A. K., & Tredennick, H. (1976). *The ethics of Aristotle: The Nicomachean ethics.* Harmondsworth, NY: Penguin Classics.
Bacal, R., & Associates. (2012). *The organizational conflict: The good, the bad, and the ugly.* Retrieved June 18, 2016 from http:www.work911.com/conflict/carticles/orgcon.htm.
Counts, G. S. (1978). *Dare the schools build a new social order?* Carbondale, IL: Southern Illinois University Press.
deMarrais, K. B., & LeCompte, M. D. (1995). *The way schools work: A sociological analysis of education* (2nd ed.). White Plains, NY: Longman Publishers.
Dewey, J. (1916). *Democracy and education: An introduction to the philosophy of education.* New York: Macmillan.
Dewey, J. (1938). *Experience and education.* New York: Simon and Schuster.
International Reading Association (2003). Family-school partnerships: Essentials elements of literacy instruction in the United States [Brochure]. Newark, DE: International Reading Association.
Jawaorski, J. (1998). *Synchronicity, the inner path of leadership.* San Francisco, CA: Berrett-Koehler Publishers, Inc.
Reed, R. F., & Johnson, T. W. (Eds.). (1996). *Philosophical documents in education.* White Plains, NY: Longman Publishers, Inc.
Robinson, K. (2015). Q&A with Sir Ken Robinson: Education has to be a "human business." *Education Week, (34)*31, 23.
Smith, H. M., & Humberstone, E. (2015). Partnerships for education transformation. *School Business Affairs,* 81, 5.
Tuomi, I., & Miller, R. (2011). Learning and education after the industrial age. Retrieved July 15, 2015 from http://www.meaningprocessing.com/personalPages/tuomi/articles/LearningAndEducationAfterTheIndustrialAge.pdf
Tyack, D. B. (1976). Ways of seeing: An essay on the history of compulsory schooling. *Harvard Educational Review, (46)* 3, 355-89.
Tyack, D. B. (1988). Ways of seeing: An essay on the history of compulsory schooling. In R. M. Jaeger (Ed.), Complementary methods for research in education (pp. 24-59). Washington, DC: American Educational Research Association.
Willis, P. E. (1977). *Learning to labor: How working class kids get working class jobs.* New York City, NY: Columbia University Press.

Appendix A: Discussion Protocol

Christopher Phillips's (2001) originally established Socrates Cafés as open-invitation discussion groups that typically met in coffee shops, libraries, schools, and other public settings as a way to engage multiple voices in critical thinking and civil discourse about complex topics. This format has been adapted for a variety of other settings, including online environments. It has also been adapted to include scaffolding of critical thinking instruction (Anderson & Piro, 2015, 2014, 2013; Piro & Anderson, 2016, 2015).

Socrates Café discussions rely heavily on Socratic questioning as the primary method to demonstrate critical thinking. Critical thinking via Socratic questioning can be scaffolded and facilitated by the Universal Intellectual Standards (Elder & Paul, 2008).

There are three steps to the Socrates Café Protocol:

1. READ (or LISTEN)
2. REFLECT
3. RESPOND

1. READ (or LISTEN): Discussions begin with a topic and at least one open-ended question. The topic(s) and open-ended question(s) are typically connected to course readings, a film, a presentation, a preliminary discussion, etc. READ or LISTEN carefully during this time.
2. REFLECT: As you read or listened, did you pick up on any patterns or trends that seemed to demonstrate biases or unexamined assumptions? Were there key issues or points that needed further explanation or clarification? Did the content or perspectives appear to be one-sided?

Make note of these observations and reflections. Resist the temptation to be so critical that you protect yourself from change or the opportunity to learn something new. Sometimes critical thinking can be too critical (Wexler, 2014).
3. RESPOND: Refer to the Intellectual Standards Quick Reference Guide to determine which Intellectual Standards best address your reflections. Contribute to the discussion by responding with additional questions from a variety of the Intellectual Standards that seek clarification, dig deeper, probe assumptions, offer a different perspective, etc. Responses should be professional and respectful, and should be supported by research, the text, or a valid source rather than be limited to opinions or experiences.

REFERENCES

Anderson, G., & Piro, J. (2015). Developing teacher dispositions in Socrates Café: Implications for English language learners. In Cowart, M.T. and Anderson, G. (Eds.) *Professional Practice in Diverse Settings: Attitudes and Dispositions That Facilitate Success.* Arlington, VA: Canh Nam Publishers, Inc.

Anderson, G., & Piro, J. (2014b). Conversations in Socrates Café: Scaffolding critical thinking via Socratic questioning and dialogues. *New Horizons for Learning, 11*(1), 1-9.

Anderson, G., & Piro, J. (2013, Fall). The Socrates café is now open: Scaffolding critical analysis within a cooperative activity. In Cowart, M.T. and Anderson, G. (Eds.) *Teaching and Leading in Diverse Schools.* Arlington, VA: Canh Nam Publishers, Inc.

Elder, L., & Paul, R. (2008). *Intellectual standards: The words that name them and the criteria that define them.* Dillon Beach, CA: Foundation for Critical Thinking.

Phillips, C. (2001). *Socrates café: A fresh taste of philosophy.* New York, NY: Norton.

Piro, J., & Anderson, G. (2016). A typology for an online Socrates café. *Teachers College Record. 118*(7). Retrieved from http://www.tcrecord.org/Content.asp?ContentId=19365.

Piro, J., & Anderson, G. (2015). Discussions in a Socrates café: Implications for critical thinking in teacher education. *Action in Teacher Education, 37*(2), 1-19. DOI: 10.1080/01626620.2015.1048009.

Wexler, E. (2014, May 30). Can critical thinking be too critical? [Blog post]. Retrieved from http://blogs.edweek.org/teachers/teaching_now/2014/05/can_critical_thinking_be_too_critical.html

Appendix B: Universal Intellectual Standards Quick Reference Guide

Clarity

>Could you elaborate further?
>Could you give me an example?
>Could you illustrate what you mean?

Accuracy

>How could we check on that?
>How could we find out if that is true?
>How could we verify or test that?

Precision

>Could you be more specific?
>Could you give me more details?
>Could you be more exact?

Relevance

>How does that relate to the problem?
>How does that bear on the question?
>How does that help us with the issue?

Depth

>What factors make this a difficult problem?
>What are some of the complexities of this question?

What are some of the difficulties we need to deal with?

Breadth

Do we need to look at this from another perspective?
Do we need to consider another point of view?
Do we need to look at this in other ways?

Logic

Does all this make sense together?
Does your first paragraph fit in with your last?
Does what you say follow from the evidence?

Significance

Is this the most important problem to consider?
Is this the central idea to focus on?
Which of these facts are most important?

Fairness

Do I (you, they, etc.) have any vested interest in this issue?
Am I (you, they, etc.) sympathetically representing the viewpoints of others?

Adapted from Elder, L. & Paul, R. (2008). *Intellectual standards: The words that name them and the criteria that define them*. Dillon Beach, CA: Foundation for Critical Thinking.

Appendix C: Seven Steps for Jigsaw Socrates Café and Graphic Organizer

Step One: Consider content

Before commencing the Jigsaw Socrates Café, students should be familiar with Socratic questioning, the nine intellectual standards, and basic group work processes. Prior to class, create discussion questions relating to course content. The number of students per group will depend on the total number of tasks or discussion questions. For example, in a class of twenty-eight students, seven discussion questions would result in four groups of seven students. Assign each home table a different content question. Type the discussion question using large font on a single piece of paper.

Step Two: Set the mood

Before class begins, create table settings for the groups to inspire a café theme for the Jigsaw Socrates Café. White butcher-type paper and flameless candles easily simulate a tablecloth and candlelight. Using a computer or iPod, play café music in low tones. The mood has now been set for the Socrates Café. Place several markers at each table for use on the white paper tablecloth. Clearly label each table with a number, in this case, one through seven, correlating to the seven varying content discussion questions on each of the seven tables. Place one content discussion question on each table.

Step Three: Create home tables

Group students by assigning a number, one through seven in this case, for each student in the class, and ask them to move to the numbered table. After students are located in their first of seven tables, announce the directions.

Each set of students at a table is known as a "home table." Ask a student from each home table to record a synopsis of the results of their content discussion question with a marker on the white paper tablecloth. Then, remind them that an additional outcome of the Socrates Jigsaw Café is to produce Socratic questions.

These are questions that result from the discussion of the content. Ask them to record all Socratic questions and other content discussion with a marker on the paper tablecloth. Allow around ten minutes for each table to finish the content discussion and create Socratic questions. Figure 2.1 represents a home table with four students, one of seven home tables. Each of the home tables has the same configuration.

Step Four: Designate an expert at each home table

One student should be designated to remain at each table as the expert. The expert quickly summarizes the discussions from previous groups before launching a new discussion at the table. Figure 2.2 represents this step, illustrating Home Table 1 with the expert who remained and three new students from Home Table 1 who rotated to Home Table 2.

Step Five: Rotate through all café tables

Repeat the above process, asking students to move to the next numbered table until each of the content discussions has ended. First, each home table's expert summarizes the accumulated responses of the previous groups, and then allows each new group to build on previously gathered knowledge. This results in the combined expertise of every student at the culmination of the Jigsaw Socrates Café. This process and final product reflects the voices of each participant and the multiplicities of diverse expressions from their classmates. Encourage active listening to promote a diversity of perspectives among students. Figure 2.3 represents the rotation of students through each group.

Step Six: Return to the home table

Step Six encompasses three phases.

> Phase One: Students will return to their original café discussion home tables. They will note, with the assistance of the expert, the changes from their original responses and the accumulation of data that arose from those classmates who followed them in the Jigsaw Socrates Café process. Figure 2.4 illustrates the students' return to their original home tables.

Phase Two: The students may view the recorded Socratic question types on the tablecloth from the home table rotation process and code them, based upon the sample types of Socratic questioning at each intellectual standard level. The students may then use slash marks to record the frequency of each intellectual standard level representing the Socratic question types and provide example Socratic questions at that level. (See Table 2.1 in this appendix for a sample graphic organizer.)

Phase Three: Students will designate a speaker who will summarize the changes and the overall types of Socratic questioning that occurred with the content question at that Socratic Café table. Each group will share a summary so that the entire class has access to the final analysis of each discussion question.

Step Seven: Discuss and Report

Ask each speaker from each home table to report to the whole class. Request that students note areas of diverse opinions and also areas of agreement with each content question. As a whole group, discuss the varying perspectives. Determine areas in which students have maintained or changed viewpoints that were established within the Jigsaw Socrates Café. Note the types of Socratic questioning that occurred at each table and the levels of intellectual standards that were produced. Discuss why specific intellectual standards were applied and others were omitted or used with less frequency than others.

164   *Appendix C: Seven Steps for Jigsaw Socrates Café and Graphic Organizer*

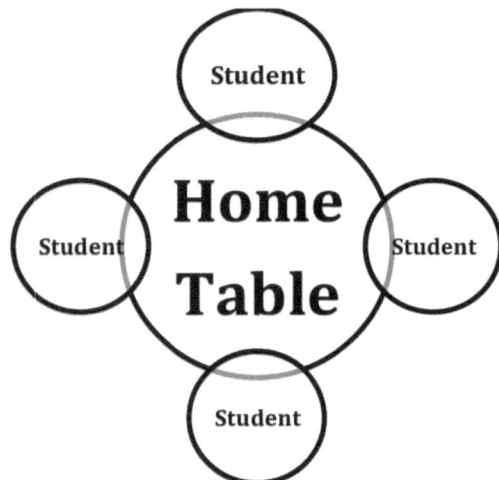

Figure 2.1. Home Table

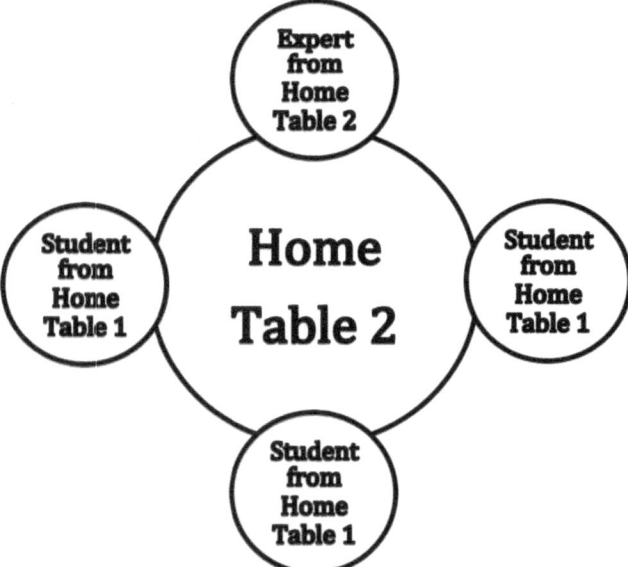

Figure 2.2. Expert with Table Rotation

Appendix C: Seven Steps for Jigsaw Socrates Café and Graphic Organizer   165

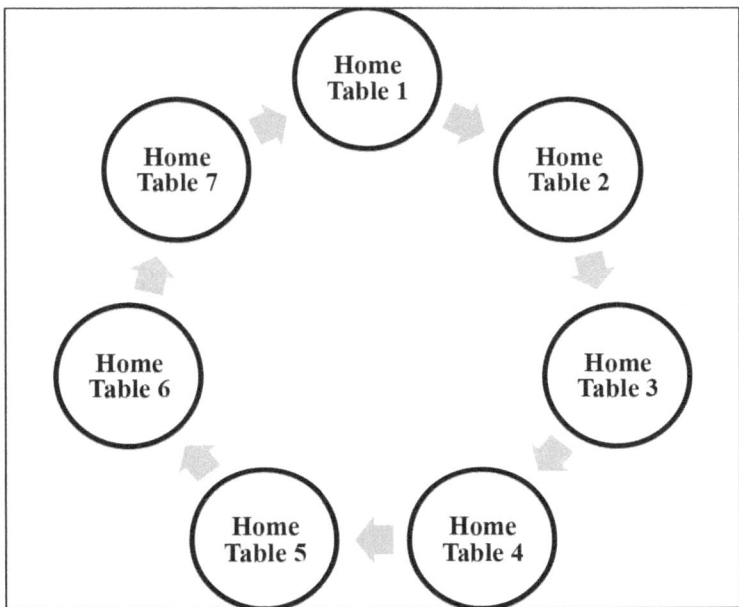

Figure 2.3. Home Groups Rotate to All Tables

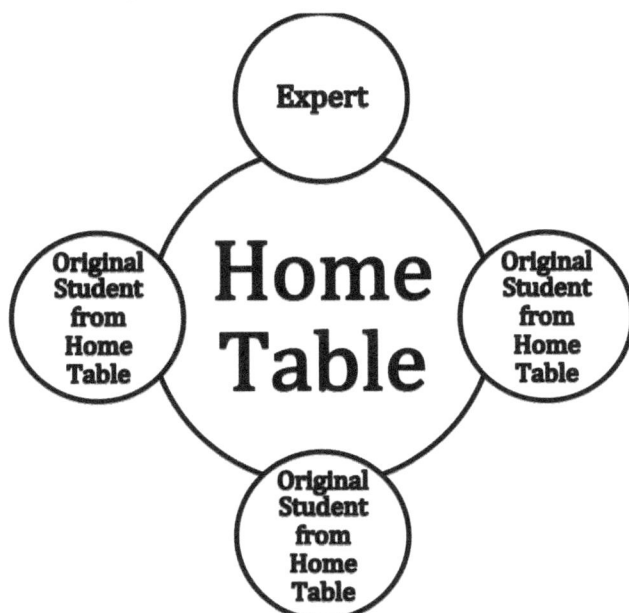

Figure 2.4. Students Return to Original Table

Level of Intellectual Standard	Examples of guiding Socratic questions for level of Intellectual Standard
Standard One-Clarity	Could you elaborate further? Could you give me an example? Could you illustrate what you mean?
Frequency Count Total for Standard One:	
Student Samples of Socratic Questions at this level	
Standard Two-Accuracy	How could we check on that? How could we find out if that is true? How could we verify or test that?
Frequency Count Total for Standard Two:	
Student Samples of Socratic Questions at this level	
Standard Three-Precision	Could you be more specific? Could you give me more details? Could you be more exact?
Frequency Count Total for Standard Three:	
Student Samples of Socratic Questions at this level	
Standard Four-Relevance	How does that relate to the problem? How does that bear on the question? How does that help us with the issue?
Frequency Count Total for Standard Four:	

Table 2.1. Sample Graphic Organizer for Student Self-Assessment of Socratic Questions

Student Samples of Socratic Questions at this level	
Standard Five-Depth	What factors make this a difficult problem? What are some of the complexities of this question? What are some of the difficulties we need to deal with?
Frequency Count Total for Standard Five:	
Student Samples of Socratic Questions at this level	
Standard Six-Breadth	Do we need to look at this from another perspective? Do we need to consider another point of view? Do we need to look at this in other ways?
Frequency Count Total for Standard Six:	
Student Samples of Socratic Questions at this level	
Standard Seven-Logic	Does all this make sense together? Does your first paragraph fit in with your last? Does what you say follow from the evidence?
Frequency Count Total for Standard Seven:	
Student Samples of Socratic Questions at this level	
Standard Eight-Significance	Is this the most important problem to consider? Is this the central idea to focus on? Which of these facts are most important?

Table 2.1. Sample Graphic Organizer for Student Self-Assessment of Socratic Questions (*continued*)

Frequency Count Total for Standard Eight:	
Student Samples of Socratic Questions at this level	
Standard Nine- Fairness	Do I have any vested interest in this issue? Am I sympathetically representing the viewpoints of others?
Frequency Count Total for Standard Nine:	
Student Samples of Socratic Questions at this level	

Jigsaw Steps, figures, and tables reprinted with permission from Anderson, G., & Piro, J. (2013, Fall). The Socrates café is now open: Scaffolding critical analysis within a cooperative activity. In Cowart, M.T. and Anderson, G. (Eds.) *Teaching and Leading in Diverse Schools*. Arlington, VA: Canh Nam Publishers, Inc.

Table 2.1. Sample Graphic Organizer for Student Self-Assessment of Socratic Questions (*continued*)

Element of Socrates Café	Self-Assessment of My Performance	My Proposed Areas of Growth
Dialogue I participated in the Socrates Café by engaging in dialogue.		
Socratic Questioning I participated in the Socrates Café by engaging in Socratic Questioning.		
Use of Intellectual Standards I used varying levels of Socratic Questioning by addressing the Intellectual Standards.		
Scholarliness I used the text or other readings to support my critical analysis of the issue.		
Interactions I participated and listened.		
Dispositions I displayed respect for others' positions. I displayed a problem-solving orientation.		

Table 2.2. Self-Assessment Exit Ticket for Socrates Café Discussion

Index

ABA. *See* Applied Behavior Analysis
academic achievement: benchmark assessment tests for, 4–5; of ELLs, 32, 39; paths of, 36; school purpose of, 151
Academic Excellence Indicator System (AEIS) reports, 126
Accountability Rating System: critical thinking influenced by, 18; for Hollyhill High School, 18; performance measure subsets of, 126
accreditation process, 58
Adler, Mortimore, 150
administration: of American international school, 51–52; CRT influenced by, 41; difficult situations of, 60; Educator Code of Ethics by, 63; ethical conduct of, 12, 130–131, 132, 140–141; first year teacher supported by, 76; hiring by, 83–84; insubordination addressed by, 63; public trust of, 138, 139; by Smith, 49–50; of Stromberg Elementary, 125; termination by, 64; vacation of, 64; walkthrough by, 127, 129, 131–132. *See also* University administrator
Admission, Review, and Dismissal (ARD) meeting: ABA for, 107–108; district services denied from, 107; parental anxiety strategies for, 114
AEIS. *See* Academic Excellence Indicator System

Alford (teacher), 27
American international school: administration of, 51–52; demographics of, 50–51; school community of, 52; school director of, 50; in West Africa, 50
"application boxes", 81
Applied Behavior Analysis (ABA), 107–108
ARD. *See* Admission, Review, and Dismissal
Aristotle, 149
ASD. *See* autism spectrum disorder
assessment measure: of Alford, 27; meeting expectations for, 117. *See also* benchmark assessment tests; formative assessment; self-assessment; Transdisciplinary Play-Based Assessment
athletic/activities coordinator: authority problem of, 53; Board of Directors for, 52; hiring of, 52; insubordination of, 53–54; reinstatement of, 56; school community for, 52–53, 62; termination of, 55, 55–56; unprofessional behavior by, 61
authentic learning, 88–89
authority problem, 53
autism specialist, 106
autism spectrum disorder (ASD): care cost for, 113; early intervention strategies

169

for, 110, 111–112, 113; home-school relationship of, 112; IDEA for, 114; instructional setting for, 103; prevalence of, 110–111

Baker, Susan: bartending by, 69; dual employment request for, 71–72; motivation of, 67–68; at Pioneer West Middle School, 67; second job by, 68
bartending: by Baker, 69; as second job, 68
BCBA. *See* Board Certified Behavior Analyst
benchmark assessment tests, 4–5
'best interests,' for ethical conduct, 136
Board Certified Behavior Analyst (BCBA), 107
Board of Directors: adversarial relationship with, 58; for athletic/activities coordinator, 52; for immediate affirmative action, 54–55; president of, 57–58; school community and, 56; school director and, 51, 61; termination approval by, 64
Bonham Middle School, 3
books, 37, 42
Boys and Girls Club, 93–94
bullying: counselor against, 93; cross-cultural variability of, 94–95; defining of, 94; intervention for, 96; Janice concern for, 93, 97–98; reporting of, 91; school policies for, 97; suicide from, 98; teacher influence on, 95, 97; technology and, 96; victimization from, 93. *See also* cyberbullying
bureaucratic organization: democracy of, 60; school as, 60
bureaucratic theory, 60

charter school: freedom of, 86; objective practice for, 88. *See also* University Charter
classroom. *See* culturally diverse classroom
classroom management: consistency for, 3–4; for learning, 11–12; for motivation, 12; at Stromberg Elementary, 131
command, chain of, 14

communication: positive lines of, 5; technology for, 82–83
community engagement, 146
conference: of formative assessment, 146; with parents, 7–8. *See also* summative conference
conflict, 60. *See also* functional conflict
conservative community, 21
contract renewal: of first year teacher, 3; of Smith, 58–59. *See also* probationary contract
counselor, 93
creativity: problem solving and, 87–88; for technology, 83
critical thinking: Accountability Rating System influenced by, 18; case study of, 17; challenges of, 21; in conservative community, 21; in curriculum, 19, 20–21; defining of, 19–20, 21; direct instruction for, 28; frameworks for, 22; Jigsaw cooperative group for, 24; metacognition for, 22; for opinion, 27; PISA for, 17; Socratic questioning for, 21–22, 23–24, 28, 157; teaching of, 19–20; TIMMS for, 17; Universal Intellectual Standards for, 23–24
cross-cultural variability, 94–95
CRT. *See* culturally responsive teaching
cultural awareness, 36
culturally diverse classroom, 35
culturally relevant: books as, 37, 42; ESL program as, 34
culturally responsive teaching (CRT): administration influence on, 41; cultural awareness from, 36; for culturally diverse classroom, 35; implementation questions for, 39–40; motivation by, 36; newcomer protocol for, 40; for sociopolitical consciousness, 35–36; teacher expectations in, 40–41; yearly phase-in component of, 41
cultural transfer, 150–151, 152
culture interview, 43–44
culture shock, 34
curriculum: critical thinking in, 19, 20–21; higher order thinking skills in, 19
cyberbullying, 95

Index

data team, 129–130
DATE. *See* District Awards for Teacher Excellence
decontextualized information, 87
democracy, 60
demographic information, 42–43
Dewey, John, 149
direct instruction, for critical thinking, 28
District Awards for Teacher Excellence (DATE) grants, 131
district services, 107
diverse texts, 26–27
do no harm: principle of, 137; violation of, 139
dual employment request: for Baker, 71–72; form for, 70; for second job, 69

Early Childhood Intervention (ECI): FIE from, 106; by IDEA, 104, 111–112; mission of, 104–105; qualify for, 105–106
early intervention strategies: for ASD, 110, 111–112, 113; private school and, 109
ECI. *See* Early Childhood Intervention
education: cultural transfer of, 150–151, 152; Dewey on, 149; guiding questions for, 152–153; institutions of, 150; school policies for, 59; societal expectations addressed by, 148; Socratic questioning in, 149; of 21st century, 151–152; Tyack on, 150
Educator Code of Ethics: by administration, 63; broad scope of, 73–74, 75; by NEA, 74–75; second job and, 71, 76–77; by state, 133; unethical practice and, 14, 133–134; for volatile language, 14
ELLs. *See* English language learners
employment clause, 15
English: learning of, 35; tutorials for, 5–6
English as a second language (ESL) program: as culturally relevant, 34; Hernandez in, 33; home visits in, 38; implementation of, 126; participant in, 33; simplest part of, 34; teacher of, 33–34
English language learners (ELLs): academic achievement of, 32, 39; number of, 31; parents of, 37–38, 41; in public school, 32; relationships of, 35
ESL program. *See* English as a second language program
ESY. *See* extended school year
ethical conduct: addressing issues of, 13–14; of administration, 12, 130–131, 132, 140–141; 'best interests' for, 136; breach of, 138; of hiring, 125, 141; of leadership, 134–135, 138; of Maleficent Independent School District, 141; of score pollution, 137–138; special needs and, 131; standardized testing and, 125, 135–136, 137, 139; of Struppe, 128, 130; of student personal information, 14; of teacher, 12, 133, 136, 141–142. *See also* Educator Code of Ethics; unethical practice
ethical fading, 138–139
ethical test preparation: legal action of, 133; questionable examples of, 134; teaching for, 134
exit rate, 11
exit ticket: graphic organizer for, 168; self-assessment for, 24, 28
extended school year (ESY), 108

Facebook page: about Hayleigh, 92; principal against, 93
faculty development, 18
faculty meeting, 18, 68–69
family engagement, 145, 146–147
Ferris (principal), 18
FIE. *See* Full Individual Evaluation
first semester behavior, 4
first year teacher: administration support of, 76; case study of, 3, 67; contract renewal of, 3; emotional response of, 12; exit rate of, 11; final considerations for, 77–78; mentoring of, 11, 72–73; second job of, 67, 75–76
formative assessment, 146
freedom, 86
"freemium model", 152
Full Individual Evaluation (FIE): from ECI, 106; Transdisciplinary Play-Based Assessment for, 106
functional conflict, 152

General Discussion Protocol: Jigsaw cooperative group and, 27–28; steps of, 24; Universal Intellectual Standards and, 24
Global Diploma, 19
graphic organizer: for exit ticket, 168; for Socratic questioning, 166–168; for Universal Intellectual Standards, 166–168
Greg (student): disruptions by, 6; permanent file of, 4; referral for, 6–7; school transfer of, 4; volatile language by, 8
grievance, filing of, 10–11
growth plan: employment clause and, 15; probationary contract influenced by, 10; for strikes, 9–10

happy hour: events of, 9; Moore at, 9
Hayleigh (student): appearance of, 91–92; at Boys and Girls Club, 93–94; Facebook page about, 92; negative experiences of, 91; physical altercation with, 92; vulnerability of, 97, 98
Hernandez, Diego: culture shock of, 34; in ESL program, 33; native culture of, 35; parents of, 33, 38–39; reading materials of, 33; second language acquisition of, 32, 36; teenage life of, 33
higher order thinking skills, 19
hiring: by administration, 83–84; of athletic/activities coordinator, 52; ethical conduct of, 125, 141; ethical fading of, 138–139; process of, 89; of Struppe, 126, 129, 130
Hollyhill High School: Accountability Rating System for, 18; Global Diploma of, 19; school year kick-off of, 17–18
home-school relationship, 112
home table rotation, of Jigsaw cooperative group, 164–165
home visits, 38

IDEA. *See* Individuals with Disabilities Education Act
incident reporting, 14
Individuals with Disabilities Education Act (IDEA): for ASD, 114; ECI by, 104, 111–112; for public school, 112
insubordination: administration addressing of, 63; of athletic/activities coordinator, 53–54
International Reading Association, 146
international school: characteristics of, 49; principal of, 49
intervention: for bullying, 96; by SST meeting, 118–119. *See also* Early Childhood Intervention (ECI); early intervention strategies
interview, 42–43. *See also* culture interview
issues analysis chart, 148

Janice (Hayleigh's mother), 93, 97–98
Jigsaw cooperative group: for critical thinking, 24; General Discussion Protocol and, 27–28; home table rotation of, 164–165; seven steps for, 161–163

Klein (teacher), 8–9

Lake Hollow Middle School: issues analysis chart for, 148; parental involvement in, 146; project management framework for, 147–148
leadership: ethical conduct of, 134–135, 138; by principal, 59–60; school environment influenced by, 60
learning: classroom management for, 11–12; of English, 35; technology for, 82. *See also* authentic learning
Learning to Labour (Willis), 150

maladjustment, 95
Maleficent Independent School District, 141
math: at Bonham Middle School, 3; tutorials for, 5–6
MDO. *See* Mother's Day Out
mentoring: assignment of, 14; of first year teacher, 11, 72–73; lack of, 3, 69; of Moore, 8; for volatile language, 13
metacognition, 22
Moore (teacher): at happy hour, 9; mentoring of, 8; volatile language by, 7, 8
moral turpitude, 77

Mother's Day Out (MDO) program, 107
motivation: of Baker, 67–68; classroom management for, 12; by CRT, 36
Murray (teacher), 28

National Education Association (NEA), 74–75
native culture, 35
NEA. *See* National Education Association
newcomer protocol, 40

objective practice: for charter school, 88; of PBL, 85
Olweus Bullying Prevention Program, 96
open-ended questions, 27
opinion, critical thinking for, 27

Paideia Proposal, 150
parental anxiety strategies, 114
parental involvement: International Reading Association for, 146; in Lake Hollow Middle School, 146; program planning by, 154
parents: conference with, 7–8; of ELLs, 37–38, 41; of Hernandez, 33, 38–39; of Smithville Elementary, 117
Parent–Teachers Association (PTA): of school community, 64; on termination, 56
PBL. *See* project-based learning
performance feedback, 10
permanent file, 4
Phillips, Christopher, 22, 157
philosophers, 149
physical altercation, 92
Pioneer West Middle School: Baker at, 67; on second job, 71
PISA. *See* Program for International Student Assessment
Plato, 149
political asylum, 32
PPCD. *See* Pre-School Program for Children with Disabilities
pragmatists, 88
prepping, for school year, 3
pre-requisites, 154
pre-school, 108–109
Pre-School Program for Children with Disabilities (PPCD): placement in, 108; social interaction of, 108
principal: against Facebook page, 93; for family engagement, 145, 146–147; of international school, 49; leadership by, 59–60; role of, 145; at strip club, 71
private school: dilemma of, 112; early intervention strategies and, 109; for pre-school, 108–109
private therapists, 105
probationary contract: contention of, 11; growth plan influence on, 10
problem solving, 87–88
professional development, 119
professional ethics, 136–137
professionalism, 7
Program for International Student Assessment (PISA), 17
project-based learning (PBL): life as, 82; objective practice of, 85; University Charter for, 81–82, 84–85
project management, 147–148
PTA. *See* Parent–Teachers Association
public school: ELLs in, 32; IDEA for, 112
public trust, 138, 139

reading materials, 33
reference check, 61, 63
refugees, 31–32
reprimanding, 14
Response to Intervention (RTI): essential components of, 120; implementation of, 121; state test and, 119–120; teacher knowledge of, 118; tier interventions of, 121; universal screener for, 120

safety, 61, 63
school: academic achievement of, 151; as bureaucratic organization, 60; functional conflict of, 152; pre-requisites for, 154; special needs in, 103. *See also* American international school; international school; pre-school; private school; public school
school community: for accreditation process, 58; of American international school, 52; for athletic/activities coordinator, 52–53, 62; Board of Directors and, 56; PTA of, 64; school director informing of, 62. *See also*

community engagement; conservative community
school director: of American international school, 50; Board of Directors and, 51, 61; first two years as, 51; lessons from, 63, 64; school community informed by, 62
school environment: leadership behavior influence on, 60; safety of, 61, 63
school policies: for bullying, 97; for education, 59
school security: for back gate, 54; for rural setting, 54
school transfer, 4
school year: prepping for, 3; termination and, 62
score pollution, 137–138
Scott, Robert, 87
second job: by Baker, 68; bartending as, 68; dual employment request for, 69; Educator Code of Ethics and, 71, 76–77; of first year teacher, 67, 75–76; Pioneer West Middle School on, 71; termination influenced by, 72. *See also* dual employment request
second language acquisition, 32, 36
self-assessment: for exit ticket, 24, 28; of Socratic questioning, 28
skill regression, 108
small group teaching, 127, 128
Smith, George: administration by, 49–50; contract renewal of, 58–59; nightmare of, 55; vacation by, 63, 64
Smithville Elementary: motto of, 118; parents of, 117; students of, 117; testing day at, 117–118
social class, 150
social interaction: at MDO program, 107; of PPCD, 108; for Sophie, 104; stakeholders for, 147
societal expectations, 148
sociopolitical consciousness, 35–36
Socrates Café: by Phillips, 22, 157; protocol for, 157–158; Universal Intellectual Standards and, 23. *See also* Jigsaw cooperative group
Socratic questioning: for critical thinking, 21–22, 23–24, 28, 157; in education, 149; graphic organizer for, 166–168;

open-ended questions and, 27; by Plato, 149; self-assessment of, 28; Universal Intellectual Standards by, 28
Sophie (autistic student): additional resources for, 105; behaviors of, 103–104; social interaction for, 104; weaning off therapies for, 110
special needs: collaboration for, 114–115; ethical conduct and, 131; in school, 103
spoken words, 105
SST. *See* Student Support Team
stakeholders: community engagement for, 146; engagement of, 146; issues brought by, 147, 149; for social interaction, 147
standardized testing: for accountability, 132–133, 141; authentic learning and, 88–89; decontextualized information of, 87; ethical conduct and, 125, 135–136, 137, 139; guiding questions for, 139–140; Scott on, 87; teaching and, 86–87; of University Charter, 86
state test, 119–120
strikes, 9–10
strip club: principal at, 71; teacher at, 71
Stromberg Elementary: administration of, 125; classroom management at, 131; demographics of, 125–126; technology integration at, 127
Struppe (teacher): ethical conduct of, 128, 130; hiring of, 126, 129, 130; small group teaching by, 127, 128; teaching philosophy of, 127, 132
student personal information, 14
students: first semester behavior of, 4; perspectives of, 154; professionalism with, 7; of Smithville Elementary, 117
Student Support Team (SST) meeting, 118–119
suicide, 98
summative conference, 10
Superintendent, 109–110

TAKS. *See* Texas Assessment of Knowledge and Skills
teacher: bullying influenced by, 95, 97; CRT expectations of, 40–41; of ESL program, 33–34; ethical conduct of, 12, 133, 136, 141–142; as pragmatists, 88;

RTI knowledge from, 118; at strip club, 71. *See also* first year teacher

teaching: of critical thinking, 19–20; for ethical test preparation, 134; professional ethics in, 136–137; standardized testing and, 86–87

teaching philosophy, 127, 132

technology: bullying and, 96; for communication, 82–83; creativity for, 83; for learning, 82; Stromberg Elementary integration of, 127; for University Charter, 82

termination: by administration, 64; of athletic/activities coordinator, 55, 55–56; Board of Directors approval of, 64; of employee, 62; by moral turpitude, 77; PTA on, 56; reversal of, 57; school year and, 62; second job influence on, 72

testing day, 117–118

Texas Assessment of Knowledge and Skills (TAKS), 126

thinking, levels of, 22

TIMMS. *See* Trends in International Mathematics and Science Study

Transdisciplinary Play-Based Assessment, 106

Trends in International Mathematics and Science Study (TIMMS), 17

tutorials, 5–6

21st century, education of, 151–152

Tyack, David, 150

unaccompanied alien children (UACs), 32

unethical practice, 14, 133–134

Universal Intellectual Standards: for critical thinking, 23–24; General Discussion Protocol and, 24; graphic organizer for, 166–168; Murray discussion of, 28; questions for, 23, 25–26; quick reference guide for, 159–160; Socrates Café and, 23; by Socratic questioning, 28

universal screener, 120

University administrator, 81

University Charter: "application boxes" of, 81; for PBL, 81–82, 84–85; standardized testing of, 86; technology for, 82

unprofessional behavior, 61

vacation: of administration, 64; by Smith, 63, 64

victimization: from bullying, 93; maladjustment and, 95

volatile language: Educator Code of Ethics for, 14; by Greg, 8; mentoring for, 13; by Moore, 7, 8

walkthrough, 127, 129, 131–132

West Africa, 50

Willis, Paul, 150

About the Editors

Rebecca R. Fredrickson, Ed.D., is an associate professor of teacher education at Texas Woman's University. Some of her publications include her work with using *Poetics* in the university classroom and for her work using experiential learning activities with collegiate preservice teachers.

Laura Trujillo-Jenks, Ph.D., is a graduate of the University of Texas at Austin, receiving both her bachelor's and Ph.D. in education and educational administration and her master's degree from Austin Peay State University in Tennessee. She has been an educator in public education at the elementary, middle, and high school levels as a general and special education teacher and as a special education coordinator, assistant principal, and principal in school districts in Texas, Colorado, and Kentucky. Currently, Laura is an associate professor in the Department of Teacher Education at Texas Woman's University, where she teaches courses in the Educational Leadership program and she also is an instructor for Capella University teaching doctoral courses for the School of Education. Laura is an associate editor for the *Journal of Cases in Educational Leadership*.

Books Laura has authored and co-authored are *Survival Guide for New Teachers: How to become a Professional, Effective, and Successful Teacher*; *The Survival Guide for New Campus Administrators: How to Become a Professional, Effective, and Successful Administrator* with Minerva Trujillo; and *Case Studies on Safety, Bullying, and Social Media in Schools* with Kenneth Jenks.

About the Contributors

Gina Anderson, Ed.D., is a professor of curriculum and instruction and the interim associate dean in the College of Professional Education at Texas Woman's University. Prior to her work in higher education, she served as an elementary and middle school teacher. Dr. Anderson has taught undergraduate and graduate courses in curriculum, pedagogy, educational foundations, and diversity. She has served as the program coordinator of Curriculum and Instruction in the Department of Teacher Education and as a mentor in the Pioneer Teaching and Learning Academy. Culturally responsive teaching strategies and the Scholarship of Teaching and Learning guide her research and scholarly interests. She serves on the Board of *Associate Deans of Texas for Teacher Education* and on the governing council of the *Curriculum and Pedagogy Group*. Dr. Anderson earned her B.S. in education at the University of Oklahoma and her M.S. and Ed.D. in curriculum and instruction at Oklahoma State University.

Melinda T. Cowart, Ph.D., began her career in bilingual education in 1975. She has been a bilingual educator in elementary school, an ESL teacher in middle school and is currently a professor of teacher education and coordinator of the Bilingual and ESL Teacher Education Program at Texas Woman's University. She and her husband, Mr. Ron Cowart, have worked extensively with refugee youth and adults. Her research interests include the consequences of language loss, the effective, equitable education for linguistically and ethnically diverse students, and the appropriate preparation of teachers who will be teaching diverse populations. In 2015, Dr. Cowart was selected to participate in the nationally recognized OpEd Project as a Public Voices Fellow. Dr. Cowart is the series editor for the current series of monographs on issues affecting English language learners and their teachers.

Kathy Deornellas, Ph.D., is an associate professor and director of the Specialist in School Psychology Program at Texas Woman's University.

Savanna Doroodchi recently graduated Summa Cum Laude from Texas Woman's University with a bachelor's degree in interdisciplinary studies and minor in education. She is certified to teach EC-8th grade and holds an all-level ESL certification. Ms. Doroodchi will begin her career teaching 4th grade math and science. Her teacher preparation program included several courses about teaching children who are linguistically, culturally, or academically diverse.

Karen Dunlap, Ed.D., is an associate professor in the Department of Teacher Education at Texas Woman's University. Her research interests include integrating pedagogically sound technology with instruction, utilizing data appropriately in both decision-making and instructional practice, and examining teacher-leadership identity formation.

Luz Marina Escobar received her Ph.D. in 1999 from the University of Southern Mississippi in educational administration and is presently a professor of Spanish at Collin County College, Preston Ridge Campus in Texas. Previously, she served as a tenure track assistant professor of Spanish and Spanish section head at the University of Southern Mississippi. Dr. Escobar has presented at numerous professional conferences both in educational administration and foreign language while also serving on doctoral committees.

Dr. Escobar has over fifty years of teaching and school administrative experience having worked in her native Colombia, in addition to Venezuela, Kuwait, Qatar, and the United States. Research interests include second language acquisition, Spanish, comparative education, and educator values and morals. Dr. Escobar prides herself in being an advocate for students and in requiring only the very best effort from them. Dr. Escobar is married to Warren Ortloff who is a contributor to this book.

Wesley D. Hickey, Ed.D., is an associate professor and chair of the Department of Educational Leadership and Policy Studies at the University of Texas at Tyler.

Patrick Jenlink, Ed.D., is a professor and coordinator of Stephen F. Austin University doctoral degree program.

Peggy Malone, Ed.D., currently contributes to the development of aspiring principals as an associate professor at Texas Woman's University. Her professional work experience in the field of education ranges from the early childhood setting to programs focused on doctoral studies. She has taught students from age three to seventy-three in Texas public and private schools and universities. Throughout this work as a teacher, campus administrator, university administrator, mentor and student advocate, Dr. Malone's platform has been to engage learners in current and relevant work to support the needs of all students, regardless of age or background. Her professional publications focus on instructional delivery and program effectiveness, collaborative conversations to support new educators, and transformational organizational change processes. Dr. Malone's daily focus is to contribute to activities, which create opportunities for all students to have an exceptional teacher in every classroom, every day, in every school.

Sarah McMahan, Ph.D., is an associate professor of teacher education at Texas Woman's University. Her research focus is in the area of school/university partnerships and preservice/novice teacher induction and mentoring.

Ava Muñoz, Ed.D., is an assistant professor in the educational leadership department at Texas A&M University–Commerce (TAMUC). She presently teaches online master's and doctoral educational leadership courses and co-ordinates the principal certification program.

She is a native Texan (Rio Grande Valley) who received both her M.Ed. and Ed.D. in educational leadership from the University of Texas–Rio Grande Valley (formerly known as the University of Texas–Pan American). Her research interests include gender equity in educational leadership, the principalship, the superintendency, mentoring, and teaching diverse student populations.

Joanna Neel, Ed.D., is an assistant professor in the Elementary of Education Department at the University of Texas at Tyler.

Warren G. Ortloff received his Ed.D. in 1980 from Oklahoma State University and is presently an assistant professor of educational administration and Distinguished Global Fellow at Texas A&M University–Commerce. He teaches both doctoral and master's level courses in addition to chairing and serving on doctoral dissertation committees. Previously, Dr. Ortloff served as a tenure track professor at the University of Southern Mississippi where he taught master's level courses, chaired doctoral dissertations, and coordinated the international master's principal preparation program.

Dr. Ortloff is an experienced teacher and school administrator having taught at every grade level PreK-12. He has also served as a school principal (elementary through high school) and superintendent both in the United States and at overseas American International Schools in Latin America and the Middle East for 10 years. Research interests include educator motivation, values and morals, and comparative education. Dr. Ortloff is a veteran having served as an officer in the United States Air Force during the Vietnam era. He is married to Luz Marina Escobar, who is a contributor to this book.

Jody Piro, Ed.D., is an associate professor in the Doctor of Education in Instructional Leadership program at Western Connecticut State University. She has been involved in education for over twenty-five years in K-12 as a social studies teacher and as a dean and principal, and in higher education as a professor and dissertation director. Dr. Piro has also served as a faculty member at Texas Woman's University and the University of Central Florida. Dr. Piro's current research focuses on problematizing discussion for critical analysis and civil discourse. She has authored dozens of peer reviewed articles and book chapters. With co-author Gina Anderson, she has published on the use of face-to-face and online discussions, including in publications such as *Teacher's College Record, Action in Teacher Education, New Horizons for Learning, Cogent Education,* and the *Encyclopedia of Diversity and Social Justice*

Lisa H. Rosen, Ph.D., is an assistant professor and the director of the Undergraduate Psychology program at Texas Woman's University.

Shannon R. Scott, Ph.D., is associate professor and chair of the Department of Psychology and Philosophy at Texas Woman's University.

Teresa Starrett, Ed.D., joined Texas Woman's University in 2010. Prior to that, she was the department chair at North Central Texas College. Before accepting that position, she was a school principal, assistant principal, and supervisor for federal programs and grants. During the time she taught teaching general and Title One classes, she worked with the University of North Texas to establish their Professional Development School for preservice teachers. Dr. Starrett's scholarly interests include experiential learning, reflective practice, and supervision.

www.ingramcontent.com/pod-product-compliance
Lightning Source LLC
Chambersburg PA
CBHW020830020526
44115CB00029B/96